A Lad of the O'Friels

A

A LAD OF THE O'FRIEL'S

BY

SEUMAS MACMANUS.

Author of "Ballads of a Country Boy."

"The Bend of the Road."

"The Leadin' Road to Donegal," &c.

FIFTH EDITION.

DUBLIN:

M. H. Gill & Son, Ltd. | James Duffy & Co., Ltd.

LONDON:

Digby, Long & Co.

1906

Sul ċuirear mé an leaḃar so do mo láṁaiḃ is mian liom a

ÉIṪNE

d'ainm a ṫaḃairt isteaċ ann;

Do ḃriġ go raiḃ do ċroiḋe te le gean do Ṗádraig mac na Ḃaintreaḃaiġe, ⁊ dá ċáirdiḃ simpliḋe:

Do ḃriġ gur tréiṫ dilis ḋíot féin, a ṁúirnín, i Eiḃlín Ní Ḃeirne—cé nar ḃ'eol ḋuit é:

Agus mar go mbéiḋ mo leaḃairín boċt mar ḃláṫ cúṁra ag na deáġ-ḋaoiniḃ Gaeḋealaċ atá ag a do ḋian-ġul.

Lá sul ṫugais do radarc deireanaċ ar ṫír do ġráḋa ṗreab an tnáṫ-solas id' súil nuair ġeall mé i gcogar ḋuit go mbéaḋ t'ainm fiġte leis an sgéilín dá dtug do ċroiḋe lán-ġean. Agus anois, a Ṁíle Stór, sul tá an fód glas ar d'uaiġ tairgim duit an tabartas beag so.

SEUMAS.

Dún na nGall,
Bealtaine, 1902.

Before putting this book from my hands, I wish to bring into it,

ETHNA,

Your name;

Because your kindly heart went out to the Widow's Pat and his homely friends:

And because—though you knew it not—Ellen Burns was a part of your sweet self:

And, still more, because, now, for the good Irish women and men who lament you, the pages of this poor book will breathe a fragrant breath.

One day before you looked your last on the land for which your heart beat, your dimming eyes lit up when I whispered that your name would be linked with the little story that your partial heart loved so fondly.

And now, O Best-beloved, ere yet the sod is green that presses your breast, I bring there my little offering.

SEUMAS.

DONEGAL, *May*, 1902.

CONTENTS.

ONE WORD.

Herein I do not sound the depths nor trace the currents of Irish life, nor show its billows and surges. To abler hands I leave that task.

Come, a summer-day idler, to this little tale. If here you see the ripples on the sunny waters, and hear the wavelets falling on the shingly shore of our out-of-the-world lives; and that, leaving, you carry away with you, in your heart, a little music of minor chords, I shall have achieved the utmost I attempted.

CHAPTER I.

AROUND TOAL-A-GALLAGHER'S CANDLE.

LIFE at Knockagar* was so placid that any pebble cast into the stream made a welcome disturbance. There was much excitement when the word went round that a little stranger from the dimly-known world that lay beyond our great wild mountain barrier was coming in to find a home amongst us.

There was not any one half so excited as I, Dinny O'Friel; nor any one half so glad. And this not because I had any lack of pleasure in my life, or any lack of company; for, the bird in the bush and the trout in the burn, not less than the hills and the streams, were my companions, as well as the other barefooted, gay-hearted lads of Knockagar, who ran with me when I chose. But

* We accent the last syllable.

these latter I did not always choose; for, though they appreciated the nests of mavis and leverock and partridge I showed them, and the trout pool I discovered them, and the den of wild cherries I disclosed to them, and the tales I told them by the way, and the fiery Irish ballads I said for them—still, they were unsatisfying: they could not roam the hills for the hills' sake, and a mavis singing on the thorn, or a trout leaping in the pool, suggested to them a fine "cock-shot," above and beyond all else. A cock-shot, I admit, tempted the savage in myself often—but not always. And when I theorized with my companions I had little weight because, I suppose, my coat had as many holes as any of theirs.

I knew that a little girl, and a town-bred little girl, for whom our world was full of strange delights, would be far more sympathetic than mountain boys as rough as myself. So I built many fantastic castles against the coming of Nuala Gildea.

On the night that was the eve of her coming, I sat in Toal-a-Gallagher's chimney corner, and the usual nightly circle of neighbours were gathering around Toal and his journeyman Billy Brogan, observing intently every stitch the one drew, and every peg the other drove.

Around Toal's workbench and big three-foot

candlestick and candle, the affairs of both the nation and Knockagar were nightly discussed, and I was always an eager auditor. But on this night all were busy counselling the Widow's Pat about the new-comer.

"It's a momentious undertakin', Pathrick," Toal said, as he drew a stubborn stitch, making a wry face to strengthen his pull—"a mo-men-ti-ous undertakin'. Ye aren't used to the rearin' of childre, nor likely much to be—"

Pat gave an assenting nod. He was now on the borders of fifty, and had never evinced any matrimonial intentions.

"—And accordin'ly," continued Toal, "ye don't know the grievious responsibility ye're takin' upon your shoulders."

For all his need of serious apprehension, the Widow's Pat could barely contain the evidences of the great pride he felt. He sat on the outer edge of the circle, smoking, legs crossed, elbow on knee and chin on elbow, and his kindly countenance very much concealed by a bushy beard and a droop-leafed hat. He attentively turned his gaze to each person who addressed him.

"For my part," Toal went on, "I have wan vagabone to fetch up—"

"He's a brave slip of a lad, is young Toal, good luck till him," Pat interrupted.

"He's a graft of the divil," burst in Corney Higarty, the pensioner, warmed by the remembrance of a recent rascality. "And it's the divil'ill have him, body and bones. He's a bad fowl, Toal-a-Gallagher! and small credit to either yourself or Shusie there."

"He has the heart o' me sore bruck," said Susie Gallagher, with a sigh. Susie was spinning in one corner.

"Arrah, don't disthress me about the villian!" Toal said. "Sure, every day the cock crows, the complaints come as thick as hailstones—though I've wore three belts on him in as many months; a baitin' is as aisy as bread and butter to him. As I was sayin' to you, Pathrick, I've fetched the seven sorras of the wurrl' on me thryin' for to rear up this vagabone o' mine; so I spaik with the weight of sad and sorrowful expayrience when I tell ye that ye have a momentious undertakin' ahead of ye, takin' this little niece of yours to rear. A girl, I admit, isn't as serious a matter as a boy. But town girls is tricksome and saucy, and they gin'rally have in their heads more antics than would stuff a turkey. So, Pathrick, be sarcumspect—be sarcumspect."

And Pat nodded assent and approbation.

"Thrue words, all of them, Toal," said John Burns, the tailor-historian. "Long Andy McCart of the Alt Mor never married bekase, as he used to put it when the boys joked him, a man 'ill have enough to do on the last day to rackon for his own piccadillies, without havin' to settle the score for a wife an' a *grioscan* of weans also, but Pathrick—"

John Burns as well as the Master—Master Whorisky—because they ambitioned politeness, and oftentimes Toal, styled the Widow's Pat, "Pathrick."

"—But Pathrick has a soothin' way with him, and a kindly, that 'ill be a big aid in rearin' up his little niece, and accustominin' her to our ways. I have no doubt but Pathrick 'll make a young woman both becomin' an' useful out of her. Besides, she'll fetch a comfort intil his life, and brightness to the hearth that has been lonely since his mother (God rest her!) left it, and went away."

I saw Pathrick's gaze go to the ground, and a single tear fall from him.

"Phew!" said Corney Higarty, who was a bachelor of fifteen years' longer standing than Pat. "I could rear a crowd of childre as aisy as I'd fetch up a fiel' o' turnips—an' have every sowl of them a moral (model) for the countryside. Give yerself little bother, Toal, about Pat's niece. Pat'll have my help. I've thravelled over a deal of joggraphy in me day—which is more than them only l'arnt it in school done—and I've met and made note of all ranks from royalty to thravellin' tinkers, an' he may depend on me givin' her the elements of both joggraphy an' good breedin' accordin' to the usages of polite society, if he only undhertakes the rest of it." For Corney thought they prosed too much, to his friend Pat's discomfort.

"Thanky, Corney," poor Pat said, with much sincerity.

"An' I'll give her"—Owen-a-Slaivin had begun, when they all looked up to find what a poor struggling labouring man like Owen could teach her—"I'll give her, for her supper the morra night, a brave hare I'm just afther wirin' in the Bottoms."

They breathed a kind of relieved sigh; but I did not; for I concluded that Owen-a-Slaivin was very generous with what was not his. I had often been vexed to find my snares tampered with; and I now know well the hare that Owen proffered was mine. I was, of course, far from begrudging the hare, or six hares; but that Owen should alike deprive me of property, and deprive me of credit, nettled me; and I resolved to watch him for the future.

"Pathrick," John Burns said, "larn the little girl her catechiz."

"Don't fear for that," Pat said.

"An'," John said, "if she can make a fair fist of

the readin' I'll lend her the 'Life of St. Mary of Aigypt' and the 'Seven Champi'ns of Chrissendom.'"

"Two of as beautiful books," Pat said, "as iver I heerd you, John Burns, readin' from."

"Edifyin'," Toal said, with eyes and energies on his work; "edifyin'."

"And afther she has parused them," John said, "provided she brings them back in good rotation——"

"She'll do that, I warrant," Pat said.

"And clane"—said John—for it never dawned on him that the soil of long years and many hands had completely discoloured them a generation since.

"And clane," said Pat, "as the day they were prented."

"She can then have the 'Histh'ry of the Holy Bible,' and 'Willy Reilly and his Colleen Bawn.'"

The Widow's Pat was overcome with John's extravagant generosity; for the greatest favour ever he had showed a friend was letting him come and read a part of one of these books under his own vigilant eye.

"If she's a good girl, Pathrick, and larns her catechiz well, I'll make her welcome to the 'Full and Thrue History of Irish Rogues and Raparees,' 'Colm Cille's Prophecies Unabridged,' the 'Complete and Wonderful Story of Valentine and Orson,' and every other wan of the thir-teen books, and half of 'Keatin's History of Ireland,' which I possess—that is, if she lives long enough to read them."

"Oh! Oh!" Pat said.

"Upon my sowl," said Toal, driving finally home a stubborn peg.

And each of the neighbours gave expression to his wonderment.

My mouth watered at these lavish promises. I had just tasted enough of each in John's great library of thirteen and a half books to make me greedily hunger for more — tasted them very scrappily, sitting on the end of the board whereon he wrought. But he had not looked with much favour on this, when he found me returning too systematically; and I suspected he was afraid of my mastering all his knowledge. It is true, that, in payment for some favour done him, the Vagabone (as we knew young Toal from his father and mother's christening) once purloined for me "Colm Cille's Prophecies Unabridged," which I fitfully devoured, behind ditches, and under shelter of *sciog* bushes, when herding on the dreary Glenboran uplands; whilst John, missing it, had raised over the countryside a hue-and-cry which got so hot that I felt like a hounded criminal skulking from justice, until, with a fourth of the exciting prophecies still unread, I shoved it under John's door at the dead hours of the night; and, on the faith of aiding him to rob Black Patrick Stewart's orchard, of Killymard, swore the Vagabone to eternal secrecy on the subject.

"For my part," Corney Higarty, who did not like to be outdone in generosity, said, "I don't own no books, and never did, since I stole Matthew Watt's Bible and hime-book two score of years ago, but I'll buy for her from Pat the Pedlar, the 'Thrue History of Little Cock Robin,' and I'll tell her (more wonderful than ever was in a book) the histh'ry of all the wars I fought, and reh'arse her all the strange and wonderful adventures I come through."

Pat was very, very thankful to Corney.

And Toal-a-Gallagher said, "Them same adventures and that same hist'ry 'll be worth listenin' to. Why didn't ye ever get the Masther to write them intil a book?"

"I should buy that book," said Billy Brogan decisively, paring a sole.

"And me, too, should it cost me ninepence," Owen-a-Slaivin said.

"Thanky, thanky, gintlemen," Corney Higarty said, pleased. "And it's often I've thought, meself, of axin' Masther Whorisky to make the hist'ry of me intil a book—me givin' it all in to him just as it happened, without altherin' or addin'; and then laive him to put the grand English on it."

"As it's himself knows how to do," said Toal.

"As it's himself knows well how to do," said Corney. "An' it's the proud man I'm thinkin' I'd be," he went on, with a reflective smile on his lips, "to meet the pedlars goin' round the country to all arts and parts, sellin' the 'Whole, Sole, and only Thrue Account of the Famious Cornelius Higarty, his Wars and his Scars,' out of the same pack with 'Freney, The Robber.'"

And all the gathered neighbours smiled reflectively too—a smile that, as I now recall it, signified, "A glory so great for Knockagar is possible—but not probable." Though Billy Brogan after a minute, gave it as his opinion that Corney was full as worthy of the honour as the great Freney; and Owen-a-Slaivin—and even Toal—endorsed this.

From my seat in the corner I had almost spoken out impulsively, and said, "I'll write a great book on you, Corney, some day," but the fear of a withering sarcasm from Corney checked me as suddenly.

In his young days poor Corney had had the dire misfortune, awakening of a morning after a spree, to find the King of England's shilling burning his fist.

He faced his fate as bravely as an unfortunate man might. And when he won his pension, there was not in all Ireland, perhaps, any man more heartily willing than he to devote his income to blowing into the elements the Empire that fee'd him.

Susie announced it was time for the Rosary, so Billy Brogan, little sorry, dropped the shoe he was working upon, and, as he untied his apron, in lightness of heart sang one of his thousand and one scraps of song :

" They hois'ed me off to Ballina, without no more delay,
And the usage that they give me was sevair upon the way ;
With their Orange colours flyin', and their cursed Orange cockade—
Such companie could not agree with any Thrashin' Blade !
Fol-di-dee, ol-di-dee, i-do !
Fol-ol-di-dee, ol-di-dee, ee !
Such companie could not agree with any Thrashin' Blade !"

And each of us was hurrying to be in time for the Rosary at his own home.

CHAPTER II.

A DONKEY-LOAD AND A MISSION.

I SAW the Widow's Pat go off next day on his journey to intercept the mail coach at Donegal, and take off it the expected stranger. Pat took his donkey-cart, and, as friend and adviser, Corney Higarty accompanied him. When Pat had led donkey and cart off the little lane which ran from his own small cabin on the knowe-side on to the road, he halted, and, taking off the tailboard, improvised a seat by laying it across the cart in the middle, resting upon the box sides. Upon this low seat, with his knees and his chin nearly meeting, Pat sat, and took up the reins. Corney sat beside him, in like fashion, save that he faced the tail of the cart, while Pat faced ahead. I myself held the donkey whilst they arranged themselves.

"Now, then, child," said Pat, "let go.—'Doff,

Fan." And Fan, with her clean-cut little legs and short, quick step, was pattering down the road, I running alongside, watching Fan, and watching Pat shake the reins on her in his own persuasive way, and watching Corney, the picture of lordly content, with arms gracefully crossed and pipe reeking lavishly, gazing complacently upon the landscape as it unfolded to him.

"Hi! Hi! Hi, there!" Toal-a-Gallagher ran out of his house, in his leather apron, and hailed them as they sped past.

"Morra, Toal," both of them greeted, when Pat had reined in Fan.

"Wan would think yous was dhrivin' for a widger," Toal replied, though really Fan was not going faster than my most leisurely jog-trot. "Go along with modheration, as if yous was Christians."

"It's all Fan's fault," Pat said, apologetically. "When she gets her head with her, Finn McCool in his prime wouldn't houl' her in. Gwo-o-o! Aisy with ye now, Fan!" And I had to take hold of her again to keep her at rest.

"Toal, what about them brogues?" said Corney, irrelevantly.

"It isn't about brogues or boots I've come to talk," Toal said, severely. "I'll talk brogues to ye when I'm on me workbench."

"Thanky!" said Corney, caustically. "I'd

sooner far ye'd make them, then. Ye've talked them long enough to me, God knows!"

Toal, with disdainful look, turned from him and addressed Pat again.

"Pathrick," he said, "I had Shusie watchin' out for ye. John Burns sent word for ye to call on him as ye go down. Besides, I was anxious to advise ye be very watchful of the little girl; see that ye give her a safe sait on the cart, and an aisy wan, with an arm of nice sweet hay in under her; and don't dhrive too hard, as ye're in the habit of doin', for a little town girl isn't used to bein' joulted over rocks in a donkey-cart. And wan other word," said he. "You'll excuse me, Corney Higarty, but I want to warn you not to indulge in intoxicatin' liquids yourself, nor give the same to Pathrick here; it would suit naither of yous under the circumstances."

"Toal-a-Gallagher," Corney said, "I'll pledge ye my solemn word of honor——"

"Good," encouraged Toal.

"That wan *deor** of intoxicatin' liquids——"

"Good, good," Toal said, gleefully.

"—'ill not cross aither of our lips this day in Donegal——"

"Bully for ye, Corney!"

---

* Drop.

"Barrin' the best of good whisky.—Dhrive ahead, friend Pat."

Pat apologetically shook his head at the mortified shoemaker, and drove on.

Toal looked after them in silence for a minute; and then called in very grave tones, "Corney Higarty, I shall put my man Billy on your brogues as soon as he gets out of hands a pair of his reverence's that he's now upon."

"Thanky," Corney said, very drily. "In throth his reverence (by the laive of his coat) might very well 'a' waited till I was supplied."

"For shame, Corney," Pat quietly remonstrated.

"The divil a bit of shame, Pat. The shame would be if Father Mick saw me goin' to mass with the bottoms out of me oul' brogues——. Here we are!"

They pulled up and went into John Burns'.

"Friend Pathrick and Friend Higarty, Simmyrammis was a most wondherful woman," John greeted them, as, inserting a scrap of cotton lining between the pages of a book wherein he read, he laid the book aside, and also his spectacles. He was sitting on his board, with a half-finished waistcoat on his knees.

"Who was that lady, John?" Corney inquired.

"She was a wonderful queen and conqueror in very anshint times, Corney. Pathrick, I shall read to ye all about her wan of these evenin's that ye have leisure and dhrop over—This book is a Joggraphy that Masther Whorisky kindly sent me the loan of Chewsday evenin' last, by wan o' the scholars—a most entertainin' and instructive book. It tells ye all about Ameriky, Pathrick, and about Ioway, where Condy Brishlan's family immigrated to. And there's fifty pages at the end which gives a full and complete hist'ry of every country in the wurrl', known and unknown. I was just takin' a spell at Simmyrammis when yous come in. It dhraws me off from my work, it's so entizin'."

"John," Pat said, "it's me'll be delighted. I'll come some early evening."

"And the little sthranger," John said, "which reminds me what I wanted ye to call here for—Ellen!" And the maidenly modest Ellen, whom I in my childish way thought I loved, came from the room and greeted Pat and Corney sweetly, laying in a motherly way a caressing hand on my head the while, and little dreaming how the blood tingled in my veins thereat. "Ellen, that cloak!" John said to his daughter.

"O, yes," she said, and disappeared into the room again, bringing back from it her own hooded cloak of blue broadcloth, which tied under her chin and made her look in my eyes so winsome going to mass and going to market. She folded it very carefully and gave it in charge to Corney. "That is to wrap the little stranger up in," she said.

"These evenin's—though this is May eve—often get cold," John said, "and I thought it 'ud be a sin to let yous venture the chile home without givin' her a good warm wrappin'."

Pat was volubly thankful for John's consideration and Ellen's kindness. And Corney, on behalf of his charge—for he now looked on the Widow's Pat as such—thanked both in polite terms. "In this cloak, Ellen dear," he said, "I'll make the little *geirseach* (girl) as happy as if she was in Sent Pether's pocket."

"Blissin' with yous," John said, bending to his work, "and don't forget about Simmyrammis, Pathrick."

"Thanky, and don't fear, John," Pathrick said, going out.

But as they were ascending to their seats in the cart, John knocked on the window with the hand in which he held the needle and beckoned Corney.

"Simmyrammis come through some great battles, Corney," John said, when Corney had thrust his head in at the door; "and besides, there's a power of wars ginirally in this Joggraphy; so, you might like to step over with your friend Pathrick, I thought."

"I'll be delighted, John, and thanky. Good-bye!"

"God be with yous," John said.

Ellen waved them a good-bye out of the hinged window of the room. And she smiled when Corney, the soldier gallantry of his younger days as lively as ever, kissed to her his finger tips.

Equally light of foot and light of heart as I was in those glad barefoot days, I would have trotted by them as far as the ivy-bridge or even beyond; but Corney, tempted by the sight of so much energy going waste, beckoned me closer and said:

"Dinny O'Friel, I hadn't time to gather a lock of *brasna** this mornin'; and I'm sore in need of some. If you go back like the good obligin' chile ye are, and take an arm-rope from behind the cupple in the kitchen, and pull the door afther ye when ye go out, and fetch in a couple of goes of brasna, and gather the full of the small can of *diarcant*† for the pig—I'll—I'll tell ye three stories on three nights—and I'll fetch ye a home a ballad from the town," he added.

The offer was very tempting. But,

"I must go to school, Corney," I said.

"School!" he said, contemptuously. "Schame school. There's nothin' foolisher for youngsters

---

* Dry bramble for burning.

† A flat star-like herb that grows in the ditches.

than too much school. Look at me!" he said, straightening himself where he sat—"Look at me that never went to school but three days and a half, and see me now!"

I did not get time to see Corney's point clearly, till the Widow's Pat had reined in Fan, and turning said to me solemnly:

"Chile, don't schame school. Me poor father (God rest him!) never sent me to school—never got the chance of sendin' me—and look at Me now! Don't do it, Dinny O'Friel!" There was a ring of sad regret in poor Pat's voice.

Anyhow I halted in my course, and Fan with her load went off, the Bummadier leaning eagerly towards me from his seat, and with much facial gesture forming his lips around the unsounded words, "Schame school! Schame school! Schame school!" And then the party disappeared around the bend at Owen-a-Slaivin's lane.

CHAPTER III.

THE MIXED DELIGHTS OF A SCHEMER.

As I went back home I weighed the matter pro and con.

My uncle Donald would be grieved if he knew me to scheme school. He had reared me, and could not have been kinder to me had I been the child of his loins—kind in an entirely undemonstrative way. I loved my uncle much. I helped him in his work, before and after school hours. But he struggled sorely to keep me at school.

The Master would be in a towering passion with me, if he knew me to scheme. He would thunder denunciations at me that would be all the more terrible because I did not understand them; and the chances were that he would salt them with Latin, and spice them with jokes that would make every boy in the barn laugh long and loudly at my expense —quite irrespective of whether they saw the joke or not; and if he forebore mounting me on Robin Haraghey's back to give me what he styled my "honorarium," he would be sure, at least, to warm my palms.

But—this was one of those persuasive days that come in the early summer, and sorely try the poor boy who is caged in a drowsy school; a shaft of sunshine, which you study rather than your slate, falls temptingly across the clay floor. And a wanton breath of wind, losing its way, comes in of the opened little sash, and, giving the well-torn map of Ireland a taunting rustle, sweeps out again. A bee strays in, buzzing as noisily as if it was he that made the world go round, and after a minute, finding it is no place for him, buzzes out, and away for the meadows. Then you hear cheery voices calling in the fields; and a stave of rollicking song, telling you that Mickey Toalan is on his way to the town with a donkey-load of turf, floats gaily in. Within, all is drone, drone, drone, buzz, buzz, buzz. Without, there is sweetest melody in the most common sound. In your breast is a fluttering, and a commotion in your veins, and in your muscles a fidgeting, and in your heart a strange prompting to throw off all restraint, and make one glorious burst for freedom and the green fields.

Moreover I should have a gay time gathering *brasna*, and cutting *diarcan*, down the Black Braes where the half-hidden river ran and sang, and the mating birds called, and the frightened rabbits scurried and disappeared. I could penetrate into Eamon's Grove (where was the best of *brasna*), and climb to the wild pigeon's nest. I could lie on my back in the sun, when I tired wandering, and whistle against the blackbird in the hollow below me. I could visit my snares; and I could ginnle a trout or two in the Burn. And—not least—I could find where May flowers were best and most plentiful. Altogether, if I would, I could have one glorious free day!

And—uncle Donald might never hear of it: the Master might never find it out.

Corney Higarty had an ingeniously simple plan of fastening his door when he went from home. A double cord went outwards through a hole; a long ash stick was inserted in the loop of the cord, without; and by repeated twirlings of this stick the cord twisted, gnarled, and shortened till the stick was drawn plump against the jambs and held the door as fast as ever lock could. I untied the fixture when I reached Corney's, and went into his little box of a cabin, where everything was neat and orderly as if he had been feeing a matron to keep it trig; and his cupboard—a hand-basket—hung by a string from the roof, so as to cheat a marauding rat that had now domiciled with Corney for years.

I stood upon his one straw-bottomed chair, and took down from behind a cupple the arm-rope. When I went out I fastened the door as I found it, and marched off whistling.

I got a pheasant's nest with four eggs (and it was a delightful surprise to find one so early) at the root of a scrubby nutbush, from which I essayed to break a bramble, in the Back Scrug; and a linnet's nest with scaldies, and a yellow-yornin's, in the South Scrug; and a nest of three lovely young rabbits almost fit for taking away, in the Square Park; and found a blackbird building at the root of the old ivied thorn that hung out from the back wall of Toal's garden. It was a glorious day, truly.

I carried a burden of *brasna* back to Corney's; and then went with his can and broken-bladed knife gathering *diarcan*. But I stayed at the Burn, in the shallows just aback of Matt McCourt's garden, and ginnled for trout till I got three. Then, under the boor-tree by the Dark Pool I sat and lay for a long hour, looking at the reflection of the bushes, and small specks of blue sky, in the waters; and listening to the sparrows twittering, and the linnet and robin singing above my head, and the blackbird, like a mischievous boy, trying half-a-dozen different whistling tricks, in the thorn bush further up.

But I had to get my *diarcan*. So I arose at

length, and wandered up to the fields in the open. I was not long filling my can. And in my course I took in three of my snares, in neither of which was there anything. "Owen-a-Slaivin," I said to myself then, "I'll keep my eye on you:" for I found fud, and a suspicious trampling of the grass, by the snare in Matt McCourt's cornfield. I got two other nests—a whin-checker's, with eggs; and a corncrake's preparing. I was near Eamon's Grove, so I would climb to the wild pigeon's nest. This was almost at the top of a tall larch, but I was an excellent spieler, and, moreover, for half its height from the ground this tree was heavily wreathed and festooned with ivy, which made the task very much easier. I whistled gaily as I went up, and more jubilantly still as I got upon the giddier branches. The pigeon flew away as I reached and shook the limb on which her home was placed. Two scaldies opened wide two cavernous mouths when I looked into the nest. I resolved to bring the Vagabone, within a few days, and, between us, overlace the nest with twigs, so that the mother could feed them for us but not get them away.

Then I slid down and had reached a slight fork less than twenty feet from the bottom, when I saw Matt McCourt digging in his garden which adjoined; and remembering how, only a few nights since in Toal's, I had heard him argue with the

Bummadier that on account of the lateness of this spring we should not have the cuckoo till Old May-day*. I here crouched and screened myself behind the plentiful ivy, and—for I was a good imitator—gave forth a good soft round "Cuck-oo! cuck-oo!"

"Sowl to glory, Bess! is that the cuckoo I hear?" Matt, suddenly standing bolt upright, called to his daughter Bess. Bess, with her wooden bucket, going to the well at the bottom of the garden, had as suddenly stopped, and, to my great amusement, looked underneath her foot for a hair.† But she was disappointed.

"It is, father, the cuckoo, and—God bliss ye!—do ye see how ye're looking? Tor'st Killymard graveyard!"

"Cuck-oo! cuck-oo!" I cried again, elated with my success.

I had not time, or perhaps presence of mind, to weigh the matter then, while I was being tumbled over; but I afterwards concluded it was less faith in Bess's augury than annoyance at the belying

---

* *i.e.* May-Day, old style—12th May, new style.

† When a boy or girl, hearing the first cuckoo call of the season, looks underfoot, we believe a hair of the same colour as that of the future wife or husband will be found. What direction a married man or woman is looking on the same occasion, a great journey lies.

of his prophecy—though it may have been a combination of both—which made him suddenly lift a large hard clod and crying: "Bad luck go with your imper'ence for comin' to crow at my lug!" hurl it at the fork of the ash tree with such good aim that, bursting through the thin veil of ivy, ere I had time to move or speak it broke on my forehead, after which I have only a confused idea of tumbling through air that I vainly clutched at, getting a great bump, and after a minute, with my can of *diarcan*, and whittle-knife, scampering from the grove, with Matt pursuing and abusing me contumeliously.

When I got beyond the reach of Matthew McCourt and danger, I said, "Corney Higarty, I've earned your three stories on three nights, and the ballad you'll bring me from the town."

And in the afternoon, though I was feeling not a little stiff and sore, I went to the beds of May flowers which I had located. I had borrowed Susie Gallagher's basket, and I filled it with May flowers and primroses. I vouchsafed a few handfuls to the Bummadier's as I passed. I went toward home, and laid them plentifully on uncle Donald's thresholds, front and rear, and on all the windowsills. "That's right," poor uncle Donald said when he saw me do it, "That's right, chile, this bliss'd May eve;" and I overheard the muttering of a Gaelic prayer escape him.

I went down our hill, crossed the road, and climbed to the cabin of the Widow's Pat, which I felt to be in my especial care this day; and I bestowed both May flower and primrose lavishly on his one doorstep and two little windowsills, that blight or ban might not enter there till May eve came once more.

I brought back a little load of them to Susie in requital for the basket loan. But young Toal, vagabond though he was, had not forgotten his duty; he was scattering flowers everywhere with a lavish hand. When he looked into my basket he said:

"Dinny O'Friel, where the dickens are ye fetchin' yer fistful of withered blossoms? I have flowers to smother the Queen of Spain and her Coort; back burdens of flowers.—Take in that basket, mother." And then to me again scornfully, "Get away with ye!"

CHAPTER IV.

THE COMING OF NUALA.

To my young imagination Nuala was something from another world. I had never before seen a town-girl who came from afar, and who consequently differed very widely from the little mountain-girls I had always seen around me.

Though she looked small to me, I think she must have been near to my size, and I know she was only one year younger—"thirteen years, last Candlemas," Pat told me. She had a head of heavy, curly, golden-yellow hair, that was uncommon to be met with amongst us—I think I never before saw any quite the same, or quite so attractive. She had lively light-blue eyes, that danced as our girls' slow eyes never did; and that looked at you very keenly, every time they rested on you. Her features were daintily plump—with dimples sometimes; her mouth both fine, and, for a youngster, firm.

This was, then, a little girl far above and beyond me; and I was delighted, for she would be a comrade worth cultivating—one whom it would be a joy to initiate into the mysteries and wonders of young life in the mountains—one sure to be so appreciative that my pleasures would with her be doubled.

I ran alongside the cart, just looking at her—never speaking to her. I had first espied the cart where it was stopped at the bend, at Owen-a-Slaivin's lane—for Owen had hailed them, and come down to the road "to bid the little sthranger welcome." "We're maybe rough and ragged, little Missy," Owen said, following Nuala's wandering eyes and looking down at himself, "but we're kindly. And ye've an uncle," he added firmly, "for all he mayn't look much, with a heart in him as kindly as May-day." At which the Widow's Pat hung his head, and blushed. And he said, "Thanky, Owen."

Ellen Burns came meeting the cart. She, to Pat's pride, kissed little Nuala, and presented her with a bouquet of primroses. And John Burns knocked on the window, came shuffling out in a pair of cloth slippers Ellen had made for him, shook the wondering Nuala's little hand, and said, "Miss, ye are welcome to this locality."

Their progress henceforth was very slow. For

the neighbours ran out of every house to greet "Pat's new niece." Susie Gallagher gave her a great hug that almost smothered her. Toal made her a stiff bow as he held her hand. And as his man Billy settled to his work again, after the welcome, he carolled:

> Had I Per-yu and Mexeeco,
> And goold and silver mines at will,
> I'd make her heir, I do declare—
> The bonny lass of Three-mile-hill.

Pat's little cabin had just two apartments—a kitchen and a room. He had his own bed in the kitchen outshot to the left of the fire; and he had, with the help of the Bummadier, fitted up the room for Nuala. Always Pat's cabin was scrupulously clean; but a week ago he had given it two coats of whitewash, within and without. Corney had concealed the black rafters and the black roof with a double coating of newspapers, in a manner so artistic as to give Pat unalloyed pleasure at the happy transformation, and the mechanic himself high pride. Religious prints, no less than seven, purchased from Pat the pedlar at a penny each, were tacked at intervals around the walls—"For I'll spare no expense, Corney, to make her wee room as pleasant as possible," Pat had said; and, "Right, Pathrick, no expense," from Corney. One large picture—of St. Patrick, with his pastoral staff, driving before him a swarm of hissing serpents, whilst a handsome Gothic church arose out of a clump of bushes to his right—got the position of honor above the fireplace. The fireplace was, of course, a hearth. The window was one of four small panes, opening on a hinge; and a looking-glass that cost ninepence several years ago, when Pat's mother, the Widow, lived, hung from a nail on the right splay. The patchwork quilt which Ellen Burns had made him afforded a very ornamental covering (in the eyes of all of us, no less than in Pat's) to the little square bed in the corner—which bed, by the way, was a feather one, purchased from Mrs. Matthew McCourt, and to be gradually paid for by Pat and his spade. Corney Higarty, moreover, had, out of his own pocket, bought four Delft figures, which he placed in appropriate positions around the room; and had crossed two old cutlasses beneath the picture of St. Patrick. And Pat had selected, on a former visit to the town, three rose-coloured vases, which now stood on the board that answered for a mantel—one at each end, and one in the middle—and held May flowers. There was an old chest of drawers—which answered both the purpose of chest of drawers and table—placed opposite to the bed; with a chair by it. The door, inside and outside, was freshly painted—by Corney—the mantel, the window, the bedstead, the chair, the chest of drawers. To my mind, as to that of the many admiring neighbours who had thronged to inspect it during the past few days, it was a luxuriously-fitted apartment, worthy of any little lady in the land.

When Nuala sat by Pat's—now also her own—kitchen fire, holding her hands to the fir-blaze and gazing searchingly at the neighbours who sat around, the latter all acknowledged that she was a little lady. Nuala, I remember, sat on a creepy-stool by one side of the fire-place; and Pat, who sat nearly opposite, sometimes watching her, and sometimes watching the faces of those who watched her, was bursting with pride for her. And I watched Pat and was proud for him.

The neighbours, as they came, brought some little present—butter, eggs, potatoes, oat-bread; because as Pat had had no woman about the house, and no cow (for he had not any land except what the cabin stood upon, and a few square yards before and behind it), and no hens, and lived as he did by the hire of his spade, he was very properly supposed to need just such attentions now. Pat beamed his heartfelt thanks upon all; and as he presented the comers to Nuala, was grateful to Corney for rectifying his own want of resource by adding in each case such eulogistic qualifications as "Keeps the warmest house in the parish," "Gets a penny a pound more for her butter than any other goes into Donegal market," "The cleanest fought man atween here and where he lives," "Was the snuggest-stepped girl—when she was a girl—entered the Oiliegh Chapel," "His bate never swung a caman," "Makes the best brogues in the baronry,"—which, if it enlightened little Nuala not much, brought Pat their requital in the blushing gratification of the eulogised.

"Ye'll like us better, daughter, when ye know us more," Corney said to Nuala.

"I like you very much," Nuala said, with a shake of her curls, and a slight smile. "And I like Uncle Pat." Here she arose and came and stood between his knees, and laid a little hand on each of his shoulders. "And I think I like everybody."

"God bliss ye, dear," Pat said, stroking her curls.

"With your Uncle Pat," Corney said, "ye'll be as comfortable as a cockroach in a chimley-corner."

"Though your Uncle Patrick's roof-tree be low, and his table humble, happiness has ever been domiciled with him," said Master Whorisky, tilting her chin, "and you will find it, Sunny-eyes."

She smiled delightedly at the Master, for he won her confidence and her regard when he had first introduced himself to her with one of his own ponderous speeches—how much of which ponderosity was serious, and how much facetious, no one but himself ever seemed to know. With only a little struggle on her part he drew her to him, and lifted her upon his knee, Pat smiling with proud delight.

"Your Uncle Patrick," the Master went on, "had, for a grander cycle of years than I care to say, successfully resisted the wiles of all women and Kitty Kierans of the Alt Mor:—but, despite his wariness a woman has made his house her home. We, his neighbors, rejoice in his downfall."

As every one of us knew well that Kitty Kierans, the dressmaker—Kitty Cut she was called because of her bitterness of tongue—had for many years thought fit to look on Pat with a favor, which he was as innocent of holding as he had been of earning, all laughed at the Master's sally, whilst Pat hung his head and blushed.

I felt very happy, seeing the happiness of Nuala and the innocent pride of Pat, and the whole-hearted gladness of every one at having such a pretty girl, and bright girl—such a sunny girl, come to live among them, and to cheer Pat's cottage and Pat's life.

But the happiness was near taking absolute flight when I saw no other than big Matthew McCourt stride in. I shrank back into the shade, whilst Matt went forward, and softening his gruff manner as best he could, took Nuala's hand in his big, horny paw, and shook it, saying, "Ye're hearty welcome, wee wan. May ye live long with us, and every bone in your body be as soun' sixty years from now as it is the day." He stroked Nuala's head, and backed away to sit down on my knee. And when he found the obstruction he, by my collar, lifted me into the light, as the most convenient way of finding who I was.

"Eh! It isn't you, Dinny Friel, is it?"

I had to admit that it was.

"Oh, ye natarnal villain ye! Ye scamp of the divil!" and he was shaking me violently. "Haven't ye got anything better to do, nor no school to go to"—the murder was out—"only playin' off yer natarnal thricks upon an oul' man and a sore-workin' wan? Troth, yer Masther should be proud of ye—and there he's sittin'!"

Nuala was watching my punishment pitifully, so my mortification was much greater than my bodily pain. The Master put his hand on my shoulder, when Matthew had let me go, and sat himself down in my seat.

"Dionysius O'Friel," he said, "what has been the depredation which begot in my valued friend Matthew this wrath?"

But Matthew himself told the story. And, when I not only saw the muscles about the Master's mouth tremble, but saw Nuala look at me and laugh a ringing laugh, I picked up heart, and I smiled tentatively myself.

"Dionysius, why came you not to school to-day?" asked the Master.

Then I trembled and could not reply.

"Did you scheme?"

I made no motion for a minute; then I inclined my head.

"What tempted your steps aside from the path that leads to lore and my Academy?" he said, with severity.

I told him truthfully that I had gone to cut *diarcan* and gather *brasna* for Corney Higarty.

He shook his head sadly, and he said, "To cut *diarcan*—and to gather *brasna*—for Corney Higarty! Alas! Alas!

"Dionysius, why not have ideals, and try faithfully to live up to them? Did you ever hear of Plato, of Julius Cæsar, of Plutarch, of Napoleon Bonaparte, of Virgil, of Solon, of Boëthius?"

I confessed I had heard of some of them.

"And, Dionysius, did you ever in all your life hear—or in all your reading meet—with anything to give color to the supposition that Plato ever schemed school to cut *diarcan*, or Plutarch to gather *brasna*, or Pliny, or Virgil? Fancy Solon ascending a tree in Eamon's Grove to cry 'Cuckoo,' to frighten Matthew McCourt! Do you think if

Bonaparte and Boëthius and Anacreon had gone cutting *diarcan* for Corney Higarty, and collecting *brasna* for him, when their Uncle Donald believed them to be under the Master's solicitous care, and their Master labored under the vain delusion that they were being unavoidably detained at home by their Uncle Donald—do you, I say again, think or suppose their names would ever coruscate with that lustre which has lit them down the ages past, and will light them down dim ages to come? And," he said, rising to a climax, "did you ever in all the wide pages of history read of any single mortal that ever won renown, and had his name and his fame bequeathed to the future ages by—collecting *brasna*, and cutting *diarcan*?"

The Widow's Pat, who was very deeply impressed by the Master's argument, sympathetically whispered in my ear, "O, Dinny, what did I warn ye!"

Corney, like the gallant knight he ever was, spurred to my rescue. "Arrah Masther, go aisy with ye!" he said, with a shade of sarcasm. "It's little meself knows about most of the lads ye mention (barrin' wan or two), and less I care; but this I'll say, that if they never done worse nor gatherin' *brasna*, nor committed a greater crime than cuttin' *diarcan*, or calling 'Cuckoo!' in Eamon's Grove, they'd have little to be ashamed of: and, moreover, there's men that has cut *diarcan* and has gathered *brasna* who wouldn't count it no great honour to sup out of the same side of a stirabout pot with them. Put that in your pipe and smoke it."

"And," said Nuala gently, patting the back of the Master's hand, "you know it was little Dinny that gathered the lovely May flowers, and scattered them at Uncle Pat's door and windows here, while Uncle was away for me. Don't be sore on him."

The Master was looking into her pleading eyes, and smiling, as she spoke. "Little Yellow-head," he said, "you are all-persuasive. I shall even pardon his champion Cornelius who wields a weapon that was never tempered in the stream of Logic."

I gave my Uncle Donal an enthusiastic account of Pat's new niece, as I sat by the fire with him late that night, though he was hurrying me to bed, that I might be afoot at break of day to herd till breakfast time up in Glenboran.

CHAPTER V.

A SUNDAY AT KNOCKAGAR.

SUNDAY was a blessed day of peace and rest at Knockagar; when care slipped like a cloak from all shoulders, when all faces reflected the brightness of the world, or it may be shone with the inward happiness of joyful rest well earned. And, however it comes, as I look back to that time, through the years, I see every Sunday sunny and joy-giving; and I hear every little noise as the cackling of one of Susie Gallagher's hens, or the barking of Matt McCourt's dog further away, or clean-shaven white-shirted Toal at his door giving time of day to Dan the blacksmith at his own—I hear every one of these sounds come floating up the hill to Uncle Donal's with a reposeful ring that I caught not on any of the other six mornings of the week. When

I called, too, from outside our door, or when our terrier barked, a gladdening echo came up from Knockagar. And I thought that surely nature, too, was joyful, and making holiday. That was my Sunday morning feeling, under the influence of which I loved—before it was yet time to join the throng setting off for Mass—to spend a happy hour loitering down the Black Braes and over the meadows, to take a peep at my nests and at my snares, and sit awhile to see the trout in the Dark Pool—or to visit my den of sloes, or my den of hazel-nuts, or of wild cherries, at other times—or my bird-traps, at a later season still. Sometimes I took Billy Brogan with me: oftener I preferred going along with my lively imagination only.

On Sunday evening, when the shadows got long—and they always seemed much longer on that evening than on any other—my feelings were graver, with a pleasing gravity; and I could then all the more readily sit in John Burns' among the neighbours, and hear the *Nation* read and discussed; and steal glances at Ellen as she read aloud.

I do not know what first inspired me with such regard for Ellen. But for many years it was a great pleasure to me to drop into John's and receive the tribute of her beaming smile; seeing her either go about her household duties, humming to herself the while; or seated on one end of her father's board, basting the cut-outs for him, and singing "The Croppy Boy."

> "It was early, early in the Spring,
> The birds did whistle and sweetly sing,
> Changing their notes from tree to tree,
> And the song they sang was 'Old Ireland free.'"

And it was surely no less a pleasure to go there on Sunday evenings, when, sitting on a chair upon the board, she gave to the crowd of neighbours assembled the great and hopeful news of the progress of Ireland's cause which the *Nation* brought to them weekly. In reward for her service she always got a handsome Christmas box, as well as many little remembrances at other special times, from the half-dozen or so who, clubbing together, were enabled to pay sixpence per week for their copy, and another sixpence to Conal McFadden for travelling the seven miles to Donegal for it.

Even Billy Brogan, out of his hard-earned few pence, gave a half-penny a week to the *Nation* club; and was one of the most constant attenders at the Sunday evening gathering in John's, and one of the most eager listeners. Billy did not comment much, he left that to those of bigger calibre—to John, to Toal, to Corney, to Owen a-Slaivin even, and the Widow's Pat. But when there was a ballad with a good swing in the issue, then Billy got Ellen to re-read that to him a number of times, after she had finished reading the paper to all. I always seconded Billy in this demand upon Ellen. And Ellen, tired though she was in all probability, would gladly consent. And finally I would get the paper; whereupon Billy and myself would retire to a quiet corner, and go over and over it many times for ourselves.

When Billy came, he chose a seat whereupon he could watch Ellen—just as I did. As she read he was—with chin resting on hand, and elbow on knee—gazing intently up into the reader's countenance. Billy and I were evidently two favourites with Ellen; for when we entered—and we both generally came together—she would drop the paper while she gladly greeted us, and not resume reading till we had got ourselves well and comfortably seated.

When the Master came in, though he was always very free and in joking humour with "fair Eleanour" as he addressed her, she did not make nearly so much ado. She smiled kindly on him, of course, and showed her appreciation of the facetious things he said; but she always looked a bit uncomfortable, I fancied, on these occasions, and resumed the reading without much delay.

As Billy and I walked home from John's on one Sunday night, Billy struck me as being—a strange thing for him—absent-minded. He sang snatches of "The Red-Haired Man's Wife" between silent intervals. Suddenly he said:

"Dinny Friel!"

"Well, Billy?" I said.

"Aren't you a purty good han' at a letter?"

"Purty fair, I think."

"Did ye ever write a love-letter?"

"No."

"Well, couldn't ye write a love-letter?"

"I don't know, Billy," I said.

"If a fella give in the sintiments to ye, couldn't ye put them down in good spellin', and all the rest of it?"

"I could spell them right, anyhow," I said. "I'm a good speller."

"Ye could spell them all in good English?"

"All in good English."

"Could ye—did ye ever try yer han' at a piece of poetry?" Billy asked.

"I'm not able to make poetry, I'm afraid," I said.

"Just wan varse or two beginning something like:

> "Ye Muses nine with me combine—

an' so on? Why, if I had the larnin' of you I would write poetry by the Irish acre."

"It doesn't depend on the larnin', Billy; it's—it's—Oh—"

"Ye mane to say it's a thing ye can't help or hinder, like Shusie Maguire's flat feet."

"That's so. But, ye know, John Burns is a good hand at the poetry, Billy. Why not try him?"

"John? Ah, no, that 'ud niver do," Billy said, reflectively. And then he sang softly:

"Ye Muses divine,
Combine
And lend me your aid,
To pen these few lines;
Ye'll find
My poor heart's bethrayed.
'Tis of a damsel so fair,
I swear
That I loved as dear as my life;
But from me she has flown,
And become
The rid-haired man's wife.

"A letter I'll sen'
By a frien',
Down till thon* sea-shore
To give her to undherstan'
I'm the man
That does her adore;
And if she but lave
That slave
I'll forfeit my life—
Or she'll live till she's dead,
Instead,
The rid-haired man's wife.'

* Yon.

"But couldn't ye write a love letter without poetry, Billy?" I asked.

"Ah, no, no. I'd as soon offer a man a meal of praties without a drop of buttermilk to wash them down."

"No matther," he added. "I'll look about me—I'll look about me. Good night to ye!" And Billy went into Toal's whistling, whilst I, wondering what *cailín* had found favor in his eyes, proceeded homewards.

CHAPTER VI.

UNCLE DONAL.

WHEN I got home my Uncle Donal was sitting by one side of the fire smoking. Uncle Donal seldom or never went out to *céilidh*.* He greeted me with a nod of his head, and, drawing a little stool from behind him, placed it in front of the fire for me to sit upon. "Throw a couple of turf and a junt of fir on the fire, Dinny, *a thaisge*, afore ye sit down," he said. "And what's the news out the night?"

"Uncle Donal," I remonstrated, gently, as often I had done before, "what's the reason ye'll not move out of a night yourself, and hear the news? It's a shame for ye to stick in the house from year's end to year's end."

He said, "Dinny, I have too many turns to do about the house, and about the cattle—ye know that."

* Visit at a neighbour's house.

"But sure I've often told ye I'd do them on me turn, and let you out."

My uncle gave half a laugh, and shook his head.

It was always the way. During the other nights of the week after having done my evening's work in the field alongside himself, and come home and got my supper, and then stretched full length by the hearth whilst I spelt off my lessons with firelight, he would say that I was well entitled to go where I chose. "While the heart's young, Dinny, take the wee pleasure to yourself—and it's me would be the vexed man to deprive ye of it—for God knows! in poor Ireland the pleasure of the young heart is all the pleasure wan's likely to have. Your hands 'ill be busy enough with the wurrl's struggles by-and-by. Take your little pleasure, Dinny—and it is little; and that's the way I'll be best plaised." It was so plain to be seen my Uncle meant this, that I could only let him have his own way, without argument.

"What's the news, Dinny?"

"Well," I said, "I was in John's, and Ellen was readin' the *Nation* to us as usual——"

"May God guard Ellen! she's a good girl, and a dutiful daughter," my uncle interrupted me.

"May God guard her!" I repeated from my heart.

"And what does the *Nation* say now, Dinny?"

"It gives a grand account, Uncle, of another glorious meetin' of Dan's."*

"Ah!"

"It was at Mullingar, and there was a hundred and fifty thousand people come to it," I said. "Thousands of them tramped fifty and sixty miles to attend it, and thousands come to the ground the night afore, so as to be sure of a place within hearin' of him."

My uncle shook his head sadly. "What did Dan say?" he asked.

"O, he made one of the most powerful orations —them was the words Ellen read out——"

"Ay, ay. Well?"

"He told them that they were the finest peasantry on the face of God's green earth," I went on.

"Of course," my uncle said, with a touch of bitterness. "And they cried out, 'We are! We are!'"

"The paper didn't mention that. Ellen didn't read that."

"No matter," my uncle said, "they sayed it. They always do. If Dan O'Connell told them the black crow was white they'd ax to be shown the man that ever doubted it."

"Oh, Uncle Donal!" I remonstrated.

---

* Dan O'Connell, styled the Irish Liberator. At some of his great meetings half a million people were present.

"I'm not blamin' them, Dinny. I'm not blamin' the creatures. They mean well. They think they're doin' everything for the best. They think it—they think it. Well, Dinny, what more did he say?"

"He sayed the last sittin' of Parliament, he didn't come all the speed he had intended to come——"

"Ay."

"But told them he never afore, in all his public career, saw things lookin' as rosy and as bright as what they now were lookin'. And he axed them, on the strength of it, to keep up their hearts and the agitation."

"Exactly."

"And to give him just three years more, and the support of half a million such men as he saw afore him, and if at the end of that time he hadn't forced from the English Gover'ment the key of our own Parliament house in College Green, and wasn't able to take that key and hand it over to them, sayin', 'There ye are, and open your own house!' he'd give them instead his reputation to kick football with."

"And then they cheered him, of course?"

"Yes, the *Nation* sayed they rent the skies. And Dan told them if he should live to be as old as English misrule he'd never forget them; and he'd always remember that as the grandest and proudest moment of his whole life."

"Ay, ay, ay," my Uncle Donal said. "May God

help them, poor people!—poor faithful, foolish people!"

"But why, Uncle Donal? He only axes them to trust him for three more years."

"I know that, child. That's a thrick of Dan's that is gettin' purty much as old as himself. Only he changes it a wee bit from time to time. Next time he'll be axin' only four years. Last time it was twelve months he wanted. Dinny, they say God fits the back to the burden. If he hadn't given our people the foolish sthrong hearts they have they'd lain down under it all and died of despair long ago."

"Don't blame Dan, he's doin' his best. He's got a lot from England already," I said. For I had been a diligent political student at John's and at Toal's. And I felt that Uncle Donal was unreasonably intolerant of Dan and his methods.

"Dinny, you're only a child," my uncle said gently; "and ye don't know all I know, and haven't seen all I've seen. From the days of the Unitin' Men, when I witnessed more horrors than I'd care to tell you, who know nothin' about such things—and never will, I trust in God—from them days down to this day, I've seen poor Irelan' bleedin', bleedin', and now she's bleedin' worse than ever afore." I glanced up stealthily into my uncle's eyes, and saw that they were—oh, so misty!

"That Dan O'Connell got many things for Irelan'

I'd be sorry to deny—very sorry. I was ever grateful for anything good he done. But, *a gradh*, it's what he didn't do, that I despise Dan for—what he didn't do. With three-quarters of a million men such faithful slaves till him that if he toul' them cuttin' off their right arms and castin' them into the say would melt the English hearts and wring our rights from them, they'd do it—and yet, and yet with three-quarters of a million men at the beck of his finger, Dan is still ferryin' petitions across the water, and wastin' the breath of him in a foreign Parliament, earnin' for us more kicks than compliments; and Irelan'—poor Irelan'!—is still sufferin', sufferin', and we lookin' on, with our hands in our pockets.

"Do ye wonder—do ye wonder, that I blame Dan?" and my Uncle Donal shook his head very sorrowfully. I was sorrowful, too, as I watched him—keenly sorrowful when I thought how, though he had a sore struggle enough to keep the roof over us, his own distress did not one whit lessen the keenness with which he felt for the distress of his country.

After a minute he took down our two pairs of beads from where they hung on a nail by the fire, and handing me mine, said, "It's long rosary-time, Dinny *a thaisge*."

We got on our knees by the fire, and uncle Donal

gave out the rosary in an even more solemn voice than usual. Amongst the small prayers with which he followed it—prayers for friends living and friends dead, for friends near and friends absent, as well as for those who in the world were friendless, he asked, in a voice that shook, for one other prayer which, in all my memory he had never omitted—"Wan Pater-and-Ave for poor sufferin' Irelan'; that God may lighten her burden, and lead her into the bright sunshine of His eternal smile." And we chorussed the response from our hearts' deep depths.

"Dinny me son, get to your little bed and be up in time in the mornin' to herd the cow for an hour afore br'akfast in the Long Park," he said to me when we arose off our knees.

And whilst I got into the outshot bed by the fireside, I watched Uncle Donal raking the fire. When he had placed three glowing coals between two black turf at the back of the hearth, he looked steadily on them for a couple of minutes, then slowly raked the warm ashes over all, cut the sign of the cross on the hearth stone, laid down the tongs lengthwise upon it, and went off to his own bed in the room.

CHAPTER VII.

HERDING IN GLENBORAN.

Now, to one who did not know them,—at least, to one who did not know them as intimately as I—the Glenboran uplands, where often I herded for long, long days that I shall never forget, would, I have little doubt, seem a place where Pleasure never, never shook its wings. I know Nuala Gildea thought so when I enticed her to them one evening I went to herd—took her, mind you, not to keep me company, but to unfold to her the hidden pleasures of these uplands.

I was all the more eager for Nuala to see Glenboran and love it, because she had so keenly enjoyed all my other haunts—my trout streams, my glens, my hills, my birds, my groves and bushes. She had wandered with me many a morning, and many an evening, over the hundred paths I knew and loved so well, and my joy, always great when I frequented my haunts, was ten-fold when I saw the delight that danced in Nuala's eye as I revealed to her possession after possession—for I looked on them as (and they were) mine. And the crowning pleasure of my young life was the discovering my delights to those whom they would delight as they did me. "Ah, Nuala," I said, when she had revelled in the other many scenes—"Ah, Nuala, but ye must have an evenin' with me, herdin' in Glenboran!"

"What sort is Glenboran?" she had asked me.

I did not describe it to her. I could not easily; and I told her so; told her its delights would have to be felt. But, by many fond references, and many hints, I had so fixed her imagination, that, now we were travelling there, I, laden with a weighty bag as I was, had much ado to leap the *sheuchs* and clamber the ditches fast enough to keep pace with her eager footsteps.

I do not know why they ever called it Glenboran. I never could know, and often wondered. There certainly was little of the glen about it. Hill upon hill arose as you travelled towards the mountains from our shore; and from the top of the highest hill a big plateau, a couple of miles long and a mile across, was scooped out, with just enough suggestion of a hollow to show the sarcasm of its title.

"What is it you have in the bag, anyway?" Nuala asked me, as, coming short in my leap, I and the bag rolled from a ditch.*

"Never mind," said I. "It's—it's the makin's of a wee fire and faist," and I now crawled over the ditch safely, if somewhat ignominiously; for Nuala laughed at the ludicrous figure I cut.

"Is Glenboran far, now, Dinny?" she asked me.

"No, just the top of this field, and then the top of the next—two more ditches, and we're there." For, as a burdened man should, I measured by obstacles.

We got over the next ditch, and then the second, and Glenboran in all its wide sweep lay revealed.

But instead of looking at Glenboran, I was watching Nuala's eyes to read their expression.

A look of disappointment grew into them. Yet I was not very much taken aback, for I had more than half expected this. Nearly every one of my young comrades who, after hearing many stories from me came with me here, was disappointed at first.

"Is this Glenboran?" Nuala said slowly, then.

"Yes; oh, but ye don't know it yet, Nuala. Take your time. No one thinks Glenboran nice at first."

---

* By ditch we understand a clay fence. That which is called ditch elsewhere, we designate *sheuch*.

"The day is so dismal, anyhow," she said, with a bit of a shiver, and a look up at the heavy sky.

"Oh, but that's the very reason I fetched ye this day—because it is dismal," I said; and Nuala looked at me puzzledly. "It's the more dismal the day, the more beautiful Glenboran is," I added: for that was so. Yet I could not then understand that it looked like a raving statement to Nuala.

"And the wind too," said she. "Sure, there isn't always a dreary wind like that up here?"

"Nearly always," I said. "And you'll soon know that's what makes one feel so happy in Glenboran."

"And there isn't a house nor a tree in all Glenboran, nor a bush, nor a thing—only thon wee couple of poor whins that's blowin' up thonder on the rise."

There was not a tree at all, I know. And she was very nearly right in saying there was not a bush but the whins—though there were six little stumpy thorn bushes that grew two or three feet high, and then gave up trying to grow any further; I knew every one of these six like a friend.

"Now, Nuala Gildea," I said, "you just wait. Come on with me, and say no more."

She came down from the ditch top, and followed me. I went on until I had crossed my uncle's marsh, and within it, behind a high ditch, I unburdened me.

"Come with me first, Nuala, and afore we do anything else, till I gather the sheep and the *stircs*—they've all wandered on Conal Meighan's lan'—and fetch them into the cornfiel'."

It is quite true that, though in the lowlands we left about Knockagar it was only a cool autumn day and dark, 'twas more like grey winter up here, with a whistling wind out—a familiar phenomenon to me. Yet when Nuala had run with me over the grey plain, jumping drains, and leaping the broken ground, and had collected and driven back with me the sheep and the *stircs*, and left them grazing at the lower end of Uncle Donal's cut, in in the corn-field where, while they were in that particular field, I always had to herd them, she was rosy and exhilarated, and inclined to be frisky and to whoop—as I knew she would. I produced half-a-dozen empty corn-bags from the bag which I had carried, and with the help of a thick whin-bush which grew high up and a few big sticks, erected a shelter under lee of the ditch, and both of us got under the shelter and crouched there, looking out at the sheep and *stircs* eating: and watching the heather tops and the blackheads, and the long stiff grasses all bent over, and blowing, blowing, blowing in the whistling winds, and listening to the striving of the wind in the whin-bush overhead; and feeling our frail house quake and shake; we felt, oh, so warm, and so sheltered and protected, by comparison with the whin-bush and the cattle and the heather and the grasses without, that we crouched and shrank and shivered deliciously with a keen inward delight that there is no describing. I did not need to ask Nuala was she happy, for her radiant face confirmed what her arm trembling against mine told me.

After a while we went out for another scamper over the fields. I led her a race to show her my six stumpy thorn bushes, letting her see that Glenboran was not by any means the lone place she would have it when she said there was no bush in all of it; and to show the clump of rushes in the sunken ground where I got a pheasant's nest in June: and the giant's grave, farther on: and the rampart where water hens sometimes were, and in which a brannet calf of Conal Meighan's was lost two years ago in April; and the ledge and the rush bush in which I had had larks' nests this very year—with an account of their discovery and subsequent history: and the little green nook in which Uncle Donal and myself used, on days we wrought there at ditches or drains, to sit down, untie the towel and eat our hearty dinners—farls of buttered bread with bottles of sweet milk; and the very rock, too, beside which I had once found a rusty penny, and been made happy; all these and many other as interesting spots—spots with, to me, immortal histories—I showed her, as we went, and dilated upon, till with a cheer in our throats and something akin to riot in our blood, we reached and dashed into our house again: and, wherefrom pitying the poor grasses and poor cattle with a selfish pity, we crouched and shivered with more intense pleasure than before.

"Isn't Glenboran delightful, Nuala?" I asked.

"Ay, it is delightful, for all it looks so dreary," Nuala said.

"But, Nuala," I said, "that's one of the very reasons why it is so delightful, and that's what makes one feel all the happier."

"I suppose it is," Nuala assented.

"Yes. The drearier the day and the darker, and the wailin'er the wind is, the happier I always be when I come into my wee house after a scamper over the fiel's or after runnin' out to turn the bastes back from the corn. Do ye know, there's many a blaik and cold evenin' I do be here for hours all alone by meself—maybe one of me school-books with me, maybe some interestin' story or history, and when I hug meself and look out at the blackheads and grasstops blowin' that way, and the wind whistlin' through them, a shiver just like this runs all over me, and I hug meself, and wonder if I'll be as happy in heaven."

"Ah," Nuala said, "this would be nice heaven."

"It would," I said, "it would."

And then both of us lapsed into a long silence.

CHAPTER VIII.

A GLENBORAN FEAST.

"NUALA," I said, after a time, "I nearly forgot about our faist. I always love to have a wee faist when I'm here, and the very same faist, made in the very same way, I'd like, too, to get in Heaven."

I got hold of my bag by the bottom corners and spilt its contents, which were turf, fir, and raw potatoes, upon the grass, before our shelter. Nuala clapped her hands when she saw these. Corney Higarty had long ago instructed me in the use of the flint and steel, and by this means I very soon had the fir alight and we were piling the turf around it. I had chosen the very driest and quickest burning turf, so we soon had a famous fire around which Nuala danced with delight, and when it had burnt all down I buried the potatoes in the hot ashes beneath the fire's heart; and after a while drew them out again, piping hot and cooked to the core. Then I produced from a corner of my tattered jacket, that answered the purpose of a pocket, a chunk of salt which I crumbled upon a dock-leaf, and Nuala and myself fell to a delicious meal.

Those who may read this story know, maybe, the taste of the boiled or steamed potato served up to them on a linen-draped table which groans with the weight of the other many great dishes to which it is a mere accompaniment. But, ah, they know naught of the delights of a jacketed potato roasted in peat ashes, and served with salt! Less still, such a ravishing delicacy partaken of by mortals with appetites as keen as the Nor'-east wind—eaten beneath a whinbush—and on the weary, dreary uplands of Glenboran!

So it would be wanton waste of words to attempt to tell of the delights of that meal.

"What will you do when you're a man, Dinny Friel," Nuala suddenly asked me.

"Me?" I asked, straightening myself. "Nuala, I think of many a thing I'll do—especially when I'm by my lone up here in Glenboran, and when I'm wandherin' the wood, and when I'm workin' by my uncle's side (for, ye know, me uncle Donal is very, very often as silent as if he wasn't there at all)—there's many a thing, I say, I do be thinkin' of doin', at them times. Only this, anyhow—I mane to help my poor uncle Donal, and to fight for Irelan's freedom, and to marry Ellen Burns." I had not the slightest hesitation in divulging to Nuala my three great purposes, although I had never imparted them to any one in the world before.

Nuala looked at me steadfastly for a minute when I had spoken, and I as steadfastly met her eye with mine, proving the firmness of my determination. Then she dropped her gaze; and she said:

"I wish I was a boy, too, because I would like to fight for Ireland." Her eyes were glinting as she spoke.

I took Nuala's hand in both mine, and pressed it hard. Then I said,

"Never mind, Nuala—never mind. There's plenty of us. Maybe, too, woman and all as ye are, ye'd get a chance also," I said. And I told her then the story of the women of Limerick who had so bravely defended their walls alongside their husbands, and their sons, and their brothers. "God send ye may get a chance," I added.

And Nuala, with a far-away look in her eyes, said, "God send."

I asked Nuala then, "What do you mean to do when you get up?"

And Nuala said, without any hesitation, "I would like to marry the Masther, and be a good wife to him. I like him better than any man except Uncle Pat."

I looked at her in surprise, and I said, "O, but the Masther's a big man, and he's twenty-two years of age—I heard Toal-a-Gallagher tellin' it on Monday night last."

"No matter," she said. She added, then, "And isn't Ellen Burns, that you mean to marry, a grown woman, too? I'm sure she's twenty-two, or very near it."

I was a bit nonplussed. I groped a minute for an argument, and then said, "Oh, but I'm a man," in such a confident tone that Nuala was silenced on the point.

"How do you mean to help your Uncle Donal?" she asked me.

"Oh, many's the thing I be thinkin' of doin' to help Uncle Donal. Ye know, the Masther says I'm the smartest scholar of me age in the parish, and says if I stick to me books there's no knowin' what I'll come to. Maybe I'll even be a Masther myself, just like him, he says."

Nuala at this looked big wonder out of her round blue eyes.

"That would surely be great," I said in response to her look, "very great. And I could then use grand English, just like Masther Whorisky does, and every one would be proud to be talkin' to me, and to have me comin' to their weddin's and chrissenin's and sprees of all sorts, and I'd be earnin' twenty-six pounds in a year—just think of it, Nuala, ten shillin's every week of my life!"

Nuala was astounded at such a prospect, and could only express herself by a wondering shake of her head.

"Anyhow," I went on, "I do be learning hard at my books, not knowin' what may happen; and it gives Uncle Donal pleasure to see me gettin' off my lessons by the fire at nights; and he'd sit cuttin' spails of fir and seasonin' them, for me to read by instead of always sthrainin' my eyes to make out the print by the light of the fire."

Nuala said reflectively, "Dinny Friel, I think you'll be a great man—maybe nearly as great as Masther Whorisky—yet."

I made no reply, but hugged myself in silent, happy pride.

After we had finished our feast, I went out and again turned the beasts back from the corn side. As I came to the shelter again, Nuala drew my attention to a lark, that I had started from the corn, which was now singing overhead—for drear as Glenboran was, the larks made their homes on it and rose into the grey skies to sing benisons upon it. I stood looking at this lark, which I could just distinguish, the size of a bee it seemed, away, away up; and Nuala had come out and stood by my side, watching it also.

Soon the lark got bigger, bigger, bigger, and its

song clearer, till finally it sailed down and lit on the ditchtop, scarce thirty yards away. The old instinct of "cock-shot" seized me; I picked up a lump of flint, and said, "Wait till ye see how close I'll go, Nuala." "Oh, Dinny, don't, don't!" Nuala cried, grasping at my arm. But I evaded her, and laughing at her terror, hurriedly hurled the stone. It went unexpectedly straight to its mark, and struck the broad back of the lark with a distinct thud that I can hear yet as plainly as at that painful moment. Instantly the bird spread its wings and mounted the air, singing—singing with a plaintive sweetness the most touching, methought, that I had ever heard from bird. It reached a point about fifty feet aloft, hovered for one minute, then, its notes suddenly ceasing, dropped to earth like a stone. It was only then Nuala, by a plaintive little scream, gave expression to her pent-up feeling. I had not spoken. Instantly she dashed over the ditch, and away to where the bird had fallen. I reached the spot as soon as she. The lark was lying on its side among the heather, its little legs sticking out stark, as if appealing even in death!

Little Nuala took it up in her two hands, kissed it passionately and then hugged it to her breast. After a while, aware of my presence, she turned on me a look that stung me sorely, a look in which contempt far exceeded reproach, and said in a low restrained voice: "Dinny Friel, go away with ye."

The heart was, all the time, crying in me, for thinking of the cold thud I had heard and of the poor lark's last song. Yet I could not say one word of sympathy or of excuse. Neither did I move. Nuala then gave me one other stinging look, and with the dead bird still pressed to her bosom went off toward home. I watched after her till she disappeared behind the brow of the hill.

Then I went back to the cornfield, where I threw myself down flat, with my face buried in the brown grass, and, I confess it, sobbed—sobbed for that which I never shall, never can, forget; the lark's last, sad, sweet farewell to Glenboran!

CHAPTER IX.

A LEARNED MAN AND THE LITTLE PEOPLE.

Of course, I never had the remotest doubt about the existence of the Little People, or Good People—the Fairies. I had never seen them, it is true, though with a feeling of pleasant dread I often thought that I should like to behold them some pleasant eve at their gambols. I had not seen them, but I knew every hill and every green knoll in the neighborhood that was sacred to them—every old *sciog* bush in which troops of them resided, and every pleasant hollow in which they loved to hold their revels; for, it is remarkable—and it was to me always a proof of their merry and genial good-heartedness—that they ever chose and marked for their own all the pleasant and lovely places, and the pleasant and lovely places only. I had not ever seen them, I say, but I had seen the evidences of them, and I knew well and intimately many, many men who had seen them time and again; and I had heard these men, at *céilidh* and at wake, in the field and in the chapel yard, recount their wonderful experiences to audiences that, like myself, listened in wide-eyed, open-mouthed awe.

One night in John Burns's, Ellen enchanted us all by reading from the *Nation* a beautiful ballad on the Little People, by Allingham:

"Up the heathery mountain,
  Down the rushy glen,
We daren't go a-hunting
  For fear of little men;
Wee folk, good folk,
  Trooping all together,
Green jacket, red cap,
  And white owl's feather."

"Beautiful varses," was the pronouncement of the Widow's Pat, when Ellen had finished.

"Beautiful's the name," said John Burns. "And," proudly, "by our own Willie Alligam, born and bred in Ballyshanny, there beyont."

Of "our own Willie," all were as proud as John.

"I mind the time," John said, reflectively, "he

was in the Ex-*cise* in Donegal there. I seen him."

"Boys-a-boys!" said the Widow's Pat, gazing upon John with a delighted wonder.

And all rested their eyes upon John with an admiration only less than that with which they would have looked upon Willie himself.

"I mind him to be there—though I didn't see him myself," Toal-a-Gallagher said. But he was too far out-distanced by John.

"I mind," John said, "to see him wandherin' over the hills and the moors, with a blackthorn staff in his fist, with a wee bit of a knapsack on his back, stoppin' and sittin' down here and there, on a ditch, or on a pratie-ridge, to chat the men and the girls would be workin' in the fiel's; and to ax them all sorts of cur'ous questions—about fairies, and *sciog* bushes, and about birds, and flowers, and the rivers, and the hills, and the old stories. And every hill he'd ax the name of, and every hollow, and every sthraim; and then he be to get them names turned into English for him, till he'd know in English why the hills and the sthraims were called that; and the very tears would come into his eyes sometimes at the mainin's of the names, and he'd say that we named all our hills and glens and sthraims with the most beautiful names ever was known in the wurrl'. Then he'd ax them weren't they all happy; and they'd of course tell him that, 'Yes, thank God for all His goodness, they were.' And he'd ax them could they tell him why they were so happy, and their land so poor, and them so poor an' sthrugglin' so sore; and they'd, to be sure, tell him they were happy bekase they supposed it was God's wish; a heavy heart, too, was harder to carry round than a millstone; and moreover, if they had to wrastle with the wurrl' atself, sure they near always managed to be its match—they got their bite and their sup, and what more did a King get? and there were bright expectations (thank God!) that better and aisier times were fast comin' to poor Irelan'; and anyhow that it was always happier to take what ye have with a thankful heart, and hope for more. 'Ay, that's it,' he'd say, shakin' the head to himself, 'that's it. Other people look to the earth for happiness, and can't find it—yous dhraw yours from Heaven. May God continue it to yous! And I know well he will—I know he will.' Then he'd take hold of his staff and go further."

"God bliss him!" said the Widow's Pat. And the others said "Amen!"

"What happened to him afther, John?" the Widow's Pat asked.

"He prented a book of his songs, and the people in London, they say, thought a dale of it——"

"Small wondher," Pat said.

"Small wondher," John repeated. "And then he hoisted his sails, and off to London himself, and begun to write pothry for the papers; and I heerd Father Mick tell, at the Station in Sally Hilly's, that he's on the fair way to becomin' a great and famious man."

"God send," Pat said. And the others said, "God send."

"And larned man as Willie Alligam was," Toal-a-Gallagher said, "he knew there was fairies, and b'lieved in them, which was more nor many others that think themselves l'arned do."

"Yis, Willie b'lieved in the fairies," John said.

"I should think he would," said the Widow's Pat, with a sense of relief in his tone.

"He b'lieved in them," John continued. "And them others ye mention, Toal, aren't l'arned enough to know their own ignorance."

I was very glad Nuala was there, and listening to this, for her belief in them was not as strong as I should have wished it.

"Right!" Pat said, triumphing.

"There's people in the wurrl', nowadays," John said, "so l'arned, that they don't b'lieve there's a God."

"There is that," said the Widow's Pat helpingly. Though I am sure he did not take John quite, literally. It was an allowable figure of speech, under the circumstances, Pat thought.

"And not b'lievin' in a God," John went on, "it's hard to expect them to b'lieve the story of the Fallen Angels—that them fought against God was cast into Hell, and them fought for God continued in Heaven, and them took no sides, for or again', cast out of Heaven onto the earth, some fallin' in the sea, where they become mermaids, and some fallin' on dhry land, where they become fairies, and still live in hope of redimption at the last day. And bekase they are in hopes of redimption it is that they like to do good turns to man, and be kindly to him whenever they can, so as to have him a frien' at coort."

"And for my part," the Widow's Pat said, "I wish them well—from me heart."

"So do all of us," Toal said.

But Owen-a-Slaivin raised his voice in protest.

"I amn't so sartin if all of us do, Toal, I beg yer pardon. If they wanted me as a frien' at coort, they took a poor way of comin' round me the night they tuck me, on me way home from the Hallowday fair of Ardhara, and kep' me wandherin' round me house and round me house and round me house and couldn't find a doore on me house, from midnight till day bruck in the mornin'; and they all the time laughin' like murdher from the top of the tully above the house. Small thanks I owe them; and in throth if I could put a spoke in their wheel for it, I'd do it."

Corney Higarty said, "Owen is wan of these people whose curse is more to be coveted than their prayers—and the fairies knew this."

"Owen," John Burns said, mollifyingly, "they're gay hearted, just like the best of Christians might be at a time, and like to play a harmless wee prank on a man, now and again. They didn't mane ye a grain of harm, or wouldn't hurt a hair on your head. Only wantin' to have their wee fun with ye, they made your doore all wan with the side wall."

"If they thought a sthrugglin' man come to my time of day a proper object to play off their antics upon," Owen said, "I'm sure I'm mightily obliged to them. And when I'm goin' to Heaven (as I hope I will), I'd like to carry with me a back-burden of sally rods, and help Pether to lace the lower half of the gate with them, so the fairies 'ud not even get a chance of slippin' through the bars."

Of course, we all knew that, though it was evident they had provoked Owen very much, he did not bear them half the malice he would have us, in his warmth, believe. So we quietly enjoyed his state of indignation; even John enjoyed it. Corney Higarty, indeed, suggested that it was an entirely different kind of spirit which had put Owen wandering, but Owen was above noticing the malicious joke.

"Now," said the Widow's Pat, "there was Robin Porther of the Glibe, and sure we all know how they carried him off with them wan night he was goin' home late, from Toal-a-Gallagher's very house there, where he'd been gettin' his brogues half-soled—whisked him off with them, and the first thing he knew he was at the foot of Croagh Pathrick mountains in Mayo, and the next place he found himself was in the County of Maith, and there wasn't a corner of Ireland, hardly, that they didn't fetch him through, and in the end left him down again in the Glibe an hour afore day, and it as dark as the inside of a cow. It was Conal Brishlan (God be merciful to him! he's dead since) that heerd his callin'—was wakened by it, and went out with a torch and fetched him in, more dead nor alive."

Though these stories were, in their essentials, almost ancient history to me, I would not be tired hearing them again and again. I was sitting on the board, beside Ellen, moreover, who had one arm around my neck, and patted my head and my cheeks occasionally with her disengaged hand. From where I sat, too, I could watch the expression on Nuala Gildea's face; right opposite us she stood, between her Uncle Pat's knees, and she was listening with rapt attention. I looked up into

Ellen's calm face; I took the hand of her which dropped over my shoulder, and patted it, and pressed it against my cheek, and felt very, very happy.

CHAPTER X.

THE LITTLE PEOPLE.

"SURE," Toal said, continuing the illustrations, in the way in which one story always led to another with us, "all of ye mind Pat Haraghey of the Glen. Pat, he was off in his boat wan night fishin' sprit on the Holmeses, and they bruck a thowal-pin, and not havin' another in the boat to replace it, they pulled the boat as best they could ashore. There was a wee thorn bush there, and Pat—against the wishes of his crew who toul' him it was a *sciog* * bush cut thowal pins off it, and went off again. But behould ye he wasn't half an hour out when a storm come on, the tarriblest ever wan of them had known, and they thought every minute the boat

* Fairy-thorn.

would be capsized the next. Big Jim McDade, who was steersman, he jumped for the thowal pins Pat had cut, and slung them out of the boat—and that instant the storm went down as suddintly as it had come."

"Not a doubt of it," said John Burns. "The same story I heerd Pat Haraghey himself tell, with his own lips. It was at Denis a-Friel's wake, of the Glen. And Larry McHugh of Dhrumgun was there, and he toul' us another quare passage about a thowal pin. It was wan beautiful, bright, moonlight night, he had wandhered out on his own hill, and sat down on a pratie-ridge just over the sae. And all at wanst, afore he knew, there was undher his eyes, right in the moon-path on the waters, a whole fleet of little fishin' boats, with little-sized men in them, and 'Larry McHugh,' says one of them, 'we've bruck a thowal pin, would ye be plaised to cut us wan off that little tree to your right beyont?" Faith Larry—and no wondher—was surprised. But he was never disobligin'. 'I'll cut ye a thowal-pin surely,' says he, 'but not off that tree; that's a *sciog*.' 'Off that tree cut it, when I tell ye, and off no other,' says the wee fella back to him, sharply. 'Sir,' says Larry, takin' courage, be raison he was a bit stung—'Sir,' says he, 'ye have the advantage off me, and I suppose, so, ye're entitled to talk so familiar,' givin' the lad a gentle rub without bein' unmannerly. 'I have the advantage of ye, Larry,' says the lad back again to him, 'and that's the very raison I ordher ye to cut the thowal-pin off that purticklar bush.' 'Phew—ew!' says Larry to himself; and without more delay steps over to the *sciog*, and cuttin' and thrimmin' a good sarviceable pin, throws it into the boat of the lad that axed for it—and detarmined to himself to watch what the end of it all would be. 'What's that at your toe, Larry?" says the lad. Faith, when Larry looked down, there he saw on the pratie ridge, right at his very toe, what seemed to be a goold guinea, shinin'. He stooped his hand for it, and it sort of moved about, so that his hand went waverin', this way, afther it; but the norra put his finger on it could he do. He rubbed his eyes like this to find what was wrong with them—and then there wasn't a thing to be seen on the ridge at all, at all. So he looked again torst the fishin' fleet, and, behould ye, there wasn't the shape or colour of a boat to be seen on all the water!"

"They sartingly don't like their *sciog* bushes to be intherfared with," the Widow's Pat said. "Now, there was, again, Owen a-Dorrian of Ballydivit, and bein' short of a revel-tree in his byre, he cut wan off a *sciog* bush and fitted it in, tyin' his cows to it that night; when behoul' ye, he found the cows standin' outside the gavel of the byre, but still tied to the revel-tree within, through the wall!"

"It wasn't in my own mim'ry," Corney Higarty said, with deliberation, as he took hold of the doubled ash-rod which answered for tongs, and mended John's fire, "but it was in me father's mim'ry, (God rest him!) and I heerd him tell it as often as there's fingers and toes on me, the story about Shan Ban of Clochfinn——"

"Gran'father to Jemmy Pat Shan?" Owen a-Slaivin queried.

"Gran'father to Jemmy Pat Shan," Corney said. "It was in a time of great disthress, and Shan parted with his last cow to get something to ate for the wife and weans. And there was wan mornin' afther, when he found the last of the money goin', too, and poor Shan was so heavy in his heart thinkin' of the hunger that would soon come on Maura and the childre that he couldn't bear to stay in the house, only went out up the Tully and sat down, and—for he couldn't help it—begun to cry. "'What is the matther with ye, Shan Ban?' says a voice at his side; and lookin' up there Shan sees a little red man by him. Shan, of course, was sore stung with shame, but he had to out with it. 'Me wife and me weans,' says he, ''ill soon be starvin', and I haven't as much as a cow in me byre to give the craitures a dhrop of milk.' 'Throth and,' says the little fella back again to him, 'I wouldn't wish that to your father's son—for it's him was kind in his day to me, wanst I was in a hobble. Go back to your byre, Shan,' says he, 'and ye'll find a cow there. Take good care of her—thrate her as kindly as if she was a Christian, and wan of your own people. Yourself or your family need never be hungry while she stands at your stake'; and then the little man was off. Shan, in a wondherment, riz up and went down to the house and into the byre, where what does he see but the nicest and beautifulest cow ever he laid his two eyes upon, and she, from the point of her nose to the tip of her tail, as white as the dhriven snow! And when he fetched out Maura with her piggins, the cow fillt every wan of the piggins to the *criovan* at the wan milkin'. From that day and that minute Shan Ban's luck turned, and his childre didn't know hunger more. Every year for three or four years the cow gave them two lovely white calves, the dead image of herself; so that Shan was gettin' up a fine stock of cattle. But at the end of three or four years, as the first two calves was cows now, Shan, gettin' a bit covetous as the wurrl' got kinder till him, thought he'd take out the oul' cow, as he could well spare her now, and sell her, and get a bit of ready money for her. Accordingly on the very next fair day of Glenties, Shan got up early and dhressed; and when Maura give him he's br'akwust he went, tuk his stick, and lowsed out the cow; but the minute he started her down the lane to dhrive her for the fair she threw up her heels in the air and let a bellow out of her, and away with her at a top gallop. And every wan of her calves at the same time, both them that was tied to the stake and them that was abroad in the fiel's, threw up their heels, and let a bellow out of them, and away afther her! And in less time nor I tell it Shan Ban seen the tails of the last of them disappearin' over the hills. And there he was left standin', dumfoundhered, cowless and calf-less, and havin' to begin the wurrl' over again!"

"And the price of him," the Widow's Pat said, with warm indignation.

"He got his rich desarts," Toal-a-Gallagher said. And even Owen-a-Slaivin, prejudiced though he was against them, gave his approval to Toal's comment.

Nuala was entranced with the story of the white cow. She left her uncle's, and stood between Corney's, knees as he proceeded with the tale. And when it was finished she came over and got upon the board with us, sitting on the other side of Ellen, whose disengaged arm went around her neck. She whispered to Ellen and me that she was very, very sorry the poor cow should have been treated so.

"Sure there's Billy Brogan," Pat said, "and he can tell ye with his own lips the quare passage he had with the fairies himself."

All eyes turned upon Billy, who sat modestly and quietly in the background. But Billy blushed, and said he had not a story to tell.

"Now, Billy," Ellen said, persuasively.

Then Billy blushed again,—and complied. "The raison," he said, with an apologetic smile—"the raison I didn't want to tell it is bekase I hadn't toul' it exactly right to Pat. It wasn't to meself it happened at all, though I be often temp'd to put meself intil it just for divarsion." It was evident that the seriousness of the discussion impressed Billy with the sacrilege which it would be to romance on the occasion. "But it was in my own counthry of Boylagh, though, it happened," he went on, "and to a neighbour boy named Brian Sweeny, that I knew as well as my baids. He was a bit of a singer, like meself. But the best singer, in fact, in all that parish or the next to it. There was wan beautiful song, in partickler, he used to sing sweeter and better nor the birds themselves—that was 'Maidin Oir,'* and for this song in itself Brian Sweeny was known through the length and the brea'th of the baronry, and there wasn't a spree

---

* *Maidin Fhoghmhar*—a morning in harvest.

ever held within miles of him that he wasn't there by invitation to give the company 'Maidin Oir.' Well, there was wan night, comin' tors't mornin', he was gettin' home from a raffle in a man named Cathair Boyle's of Letterilly; he was comin' along across a curragh below his own house, when all at wanst he found a lake of water all round him, and thry all he could there wasn't anyway to get out. Then he stood to think to himself, and that minute he heered a great cheer and a laugh, and a whole lot of voices begun callin' out, 'Sing us "Maidin Oir," Brian Sweeny! Sing us "Maidin Oir," Brian Sweeny!' 'Faith, and I will that, with a heart and a half,' says Brian. And standin' where he was, in the middle of the Curragh, Brian sthruck it up, and, at his very best, sung every wan of its seventeen varses; and when he finished he got a tarrible great cheerin', cheerin', and clappin' of hands; and a voice called out 'Good for ye, Brian Sweeny! It's every bit as good as we heerd tell of; good-bye, and good-luck!' and immediately there wasn't a dhrop of water around him, but what had disappeared away; and Brian walked home safe. But it was a good while again, for all that, afore he would venture to come home by his lone in the middle of the night."

"Yis, yis, they're so gay-hearted!" Toal said. "Music and singin' and dancin' and gaiety of all sorts is the life and sowl of them. Sure, I mind meself, when I was a lump of a lad, to hear of what happen'd to a near frien' of me own, Peggy McCue. It was less nor a week after she'd been marri'd on Long Micky Diver; Micky had gone over to the nixt townland to ax a day's mowin' off Billy Logue, and left Peggy alone in the house, where, afther givin' the floore a nice, clane sweep, and sweepin' the hearth up, and puttin' on a good bright fire, she sat down to her wheel, and was singin' aisy to herself as she spun, again' the Hallow-day yarn-market in Donegal. In the middle of it there was a knock at the doore, and when she sayed, 'Come in,' in walks the purtiest and daintiest little man and woman she'd ever laid her eyes on, and makin' a low curtshey to her, says, 'If it's plaisin' to ye, ma'am, might we have your laive for an hour, to hold our weddin' party here? for there's a flood in the Curragh.' 'Ye surely can,' says Peggy, lookin' at them in surprise. They thanked her and went out, and presently come back again, with four-and-twenty little couples, man and woman, at their heels, all beautifully dhressed, and gay with ribbons —half of the men playin' pipes, and the other half playin' fiddles. They all marched up and curtshied to her, pair by pair, the gentlemen holdin' the ladies' hands as they made their bow. Then they squared themselves round, and begun dancin', with the bride and groom leadin' off. The fiddlers would play at wan time while the pipers danced, and nixt the pipers would play while the fiddlers danced. Peggy, she never stopped her spinnin', but still she tuk in with her eye everything; and the like of such lovely dancin' and such beautiful playin', she says, she never afore witnessed or heerd. At the end of every dance, a messenger used to go out, and at last wan of these come runnin', and says, 'We must be off—Micky's comin' down the Alt above.' Then they jumped up and paired off, and marched past her as afore, every pair makin' a low curtshey to her, and thankin' her, and the groom sayin', 'Peggy McCue, ye have our hearty good-will and good wish. May your marri'd life be as happy as ours.' And all fiddled and piped it out. Peggy never saw them more; but the wurrl' thruv with her, Micky Diver's loud word was niver heerd to her, and a care niver bent her brow."

"Thrue, thrue," Pat said. "And them has the fairies' good wish and keeps it, will ever prosper. Och-anee-o!" he sighed, "isn't it the sorraful, sorraful, pity they can niver see Heaven again."

"Can't they?" asked Billy Brogan in a pained voice. "O Pat, but it isn't for you or me to judge that," he added, with some relief.

"Oh, I wisht, I wisht, as much as you, Billy, that I could think there was a chance for them.

But I'm afeerd, I'm sore afeerd," and he shook his head sadly. "John, here, 'ill tell ye about that—Tell Bill the story about Father Dick McGoldrick, John."

John slowly withdrew from his mouth the pipe, wiped its stem, and passed it to Billy, who, taking it, crossed his legs, and began to pull vigorously, keeping his eyes keenly fixed on John the while.

"I suppose," John said, after some moments' reflection, "it's four-score of years and more ago, and Father Dick McGoldrick was then parish priest of this very parish ye're sittin' in. There was wan night—a harvest night—he got a sick-call to Owenrua, at the back of Binbane mountain, and, as usual, he rode on an old gray mare he had—a mare he'd had for well over a score of years; and both himself and the mare were grown old together. When he'd got to his journey's end and given the rites to some poor sowl that was goin' on its long journey, he started for home again; and it was then afther twelve o'clock.

"There was a bright moonlight and a full moon, so that he could see the white Binbane road sthretchin' away afore himself and his old white mare for far enough; and along this white road he come joggin' aisily—for himself or his old white mare never hurried when they could help it—and sayin' his prayers, when all of a suddint the mare pulls up so short as near to throw him off; and, lookin' ahead to find what was the matter, he sees, reachin' from his very horse's head as far along the road as his eye could carry, multitudes on multitudes of little people on horseback, six deep; and them now standin' as still as the heather that grew be the roadside! Father Dick, he crossed himself, which give him courage, and says he, to the men in the foremost rank, 'In God's name,' says he, 'what's abother to yous? or what's throublin' yous?' Wan of them spoke up, and says he, 'Priest, we have been thousands of years wandherin' this earth now, and will be thousands more; and all that time wan great question is throublin' our minds. We want it set at rest for good-and-all, for better or for worse, now this night. For that we've gathered, thousands upon thousands of us as ye see, from all ends of the earth, to meet you, and put the question.' 'Good people,' says the priest, 'what is your question?' 'We want to know,' says the spokesman, 'is it your opinion that, afther long banishment, we can ever by any means get back into Heaven again?' Father Dick he didn't give him any direct answer, till first he prayed long within himself. At the end of that, he lifted his head again, and he says, 'Good people, don't press me for an answer to that question. Go back, go back to where ye come from.' But 'No, no!' says the spokesman, and from all them thousands upon thousands there came a 'No, no!' that was like a suddint storm sweepin' the bogs. 'We've come for an answer,' says the spokesman, 'and an answer we must get or you'll never pass here!' When the priest heerd this he was sorry. He begun to pray for another while, and when he lifted his head again he sayed to them, 'This is me answer: If in the veins of all the thousands upon thousands of ye that are here, as much blood can be found as would sit on the point of a pin, there's a hope for yous.' And the instant they heerd this, there went up from them the dreadfullest and painfullest wail that ever was heerd in the wurrl'; a blast of win' swep' by the priest, and when he looked, there was nothin' but the long bare white road afore him again."

The mouth of the Widow's Pat was drooped as he looked to Billy Brogan, and gave him a slight inclination of the head which meant, "Now Billy?" And Billy replied to him with a mournful headshake which said, "Yis, yis, Pat."

Ellen had gathered myself and Nuala closer to her as the story went on. And now it was finished she touched her lips upon the top of my head and of Nuala's: but neither of us said a word.

CHAPTER XI.

MY FIRST FLOGGING.

THOUGH I do not claim to have been a model youth—I know I was far from such—I have the recollection of getting only one smart flogging.

It was not from my uncle Donal, certainly. Though I had been with him since I was three years old—at which time I was left an orphan—he had never once raised a finger to me; I never even heard his cross word; I never saw his cross look. His reprimand for my misdeeds ever was a grave, feeling word; and such a word from him was more deterrent than if he had broken sticks upon me. I know that, despite his mild rebuke and kindly advice, the spirit of mischief—which was always strong in me—moved me again and again; but I also know that after earning such censure I strove hard for a couple of weeks to live up to ideals that were, alas! too often dormant with me. And, despite the prate of the carpers who tell us Hell is paved with good intentions, I will say that I know I was better for that striving; and I do not, and never will, pin a particle of faith to such dictum.

It was not from the Master I got my flogging. I never knew the Master to flog. He punished the palms of my hands with more or less vigour at rare times, and he thundered at me in awful polysyllabic terms again, and at other times, sorer than any, he turned the laugh of the school upon me again. But the Master's passion was always more affected than real; there was more cry than wool with him; and to me, in particular, he was more than ordinarily lenient, and of me more than ordinarily fond.

It was from my friend Toal-a-Gallagher I got my flogging. For it I extended him no good will then. When I considered I had got even with him —which I did, not long after—I was gratified to an extent almost sinful. But, at this distance of time, I can afford to say I earned all he gave me, and I will admit my flesh was hurt much less by that flogging than my spirit.

The Vagabone—which was Toal the younger—in carrying into effect his devilry, had often found me of great use to him, because he found I could plan with him and originate a scheme, when his other lieutenants were utterly useless. "Dinny

Friel," he used to say admiringly to his gathered clan (for he was chieftain and despot among the youth of Knockagar), "has a head with more in it nor a comb would take out." The Vagabone, being of a martial spirit, had organized us all into an army and drilled us, with *camans* upon our shoulders for guns, and trained us to battle—sham battle he called it, because, I suppose, there was very little sham about it usually—which we many times experienced to our cost. The Vagabone had ever been an eager attender at Corney Higarty's fireside, where he listened with eagerness to the many graphic accounts of broil and battle Corney loved to retail by way of treat to the neighbours who favoured his hearth with their kindly presence. After hearing Corney's description of a battle, the Vagabone always took an early opportunity of calling upon his vassals and re-enacting the engagement.

Then, too, on one of many occasions on which the Vagabone had been on his banishment away in the Augherbeg country, in his Uncle Neil's (whither he always fled from his father's wrath—and strap—on the commission of a misdeed more outrageous than usual), he returned, bringing with him to me a very much-used, well-worn, and torn history of Ireland, "which gives a grand account," he assured me, "of all the wars of Ireland. While that book lasts ye, we'll have some bonny fightin'." I was hugely delighted to get hold of such a treasure as a history of Ireland. Toal was not inclined to be lavish of information regarding how such a precious work came into his possession; and, I confess, I did not show any impertinent curiosity on the subject. In John Burns' Keating I had only been permitted short indulgences; John's was only half a book besides; and, moreover, even an entire Keating omitted the exciting last three centuries of our history. So it will be readily believed that I devoured the volume the Vagabone brought me. On the very top of his father's whinny hill he would bring together his henchmen of an evening, and seat them around me and Nuala Gildea (whom I always invited and he tolerated by courtesy), whilst I read out to them enthralling episodes of our country's wonderful past. He made his lieges all repeat after me, and get by heart, some ringing battle-songs that were interspersed; and Billy Brogan, who joined us on Sundays, was best and quickest at this.

From this time all the Vagabond's hearty hatred, and all his battles, were directed against the English; and we waged again and again the noted battles of our history—not seldom with such damage to the property of non-combatants, that cranky individuals who lacked proper appreciation of military ardour, tramped upon each other's heels as they thronged to the residence of the senior Toal, to lodge loud-voiced complaints.

One of the incidents in the history which struck the Vagabone, and, indeed, all of us, most, was the keeping of the bridge of Athlone; an incident which for rousing heroism is rarely paralleled in the world's records—save by that of the half-mythical Horatius "in the brave days of old."

"Upon my sowl," said the Vagabone, smiting his thigh, "and we must have the battle of the bridge of Athlone afore I'm a day oulder. All cheered the project rapturously. Then one suggested this bridge, and another that, and a third got another one for the bridge of Athlone. "No, no," said Toal, "neither of them yous mention. We'd niver get them broken and come out alive," for every one of the bridges named were on the main road to Donegal. "Och," said one of the boys, "and do ye mane to railly br'ak them?" Toal turned on him a severe look and said, "If you think this battle is only goin' to be play-actin' I advise ye the safest way to come out of it with soun' ribs is to go home afore it begins, and houl' yarn for your mother." So it was going to be in very deadly earnest; and, accordingly, every man got fidgety for it.

"What bridge will it be then, Toal?" I asked him.

"There's no better bridge I know," he said, "than the han'-rail bridge over the burn at the bottom of me father's garden."

The idea of destroying a bridge that had cost the elder Toal much thought and time and labour, and money—the property, too, of a man so stern and so resourceful—for a moment took our breath away; but the very daring of it next moment fired us with enthusiasm, and we cheered our hero with all the force of our lungs.

"And afther the breakin' of the bridge," Toal proceeded, as calmly as if vanity was a thing beneath him, "we'll then burn Athlone."

"What do you mean, Toal? Not burn Knockagar, surely?" I questioned.

"No, not Knockagar; but we'll burn me father's hill—both the whins and grass is dhry as gunpowdher; and we'll have what the Masther would call 'a conspicuous cumflagration.'"

The resources of our leader dazzled us. Such a spectacle, too, as Toal's whinny hill one tongue of flame would be welcome recompense to us after the knocks of the battle.

The Vagabone had made a bold attempt to fire the whinny hill not many weeks before, but was frustrated by the untimely appearance of his father on the scene, and fled to Augherbeg for a term of banishment.

It was agreed that Athlone should be burnt when darkness fell. But as the hill arose right in front of Toal's house, there was every risk of his seeing the conflagration in time to stamp it out, and mar the spectacular display, and perhaps capture the incendiaries. "So, Dinny Friel," the Vagabone said to me, "as it's you has the gift of the gab, you'll go into the oul' man, and read him the Seven Wise Champins of Chrissendom, or *dhraw* him on Dan O'Connell or the Scripthurs, while we are risin' the blaze."

It was not the first time I had been chosen for just such a mission, and that I had been successful is evidenced by the embassy falling to me again.

These plans were laid on a Friday evening, and Toal notified his faithful kernes to meet him on Saturday evening in the field behind his father's garden, bringing with them their arms and ammunition—*camans*, to wit, and stones.

At the appointed time and place all were assembled, with *camans* on shoulders, and pockets laden low with stones. We were told off into two armies, English and Irish. As the second post of honour, the Vagabone would have me Ginkell, leader of the Williamites; but I would not for that forego the honour of defending the bridge, even as a private; I asked to be Custume, who should volunteer to cut the bridge in the teeth of Ginkell's cannon. Toal would permit me to be one of his ten volunteers, but the honour of being Custume in preference even to St. Ruth, he reserved for himself.

The battle of the bridge was one of the fiercest in the whole campaign. On the brave defenders for a long hour rained stones and *caman*-blows; yet they held their ground undaunted—held their ground until the bridge, whose supports were all the time being attacked with axe and sledge and saw, was ready to give way; then Toal and his Irish lads hastily fell back a moment before the structure—to the intense satisfaction of both attackers and attacked—totally collapsed, the crash as it fell into the burn being only drowned by the wild united cheers of both armies.

But certainly the most exciting part of the battle was yet to come, and was witnessed after Ginkell (who was a son of Matt McCourt's) and his Dutchmen, had thrown a temporary bridge—of twelve-foots which had been borrowed (without his knowledge) from James Griffin, the stone mason—across the burn. Then it was that the Vagabone, representing Custume, sprang out in front of the forces and asked for ten volunteers to break the bridge, or die—or perhaps both. And in another minute eleven of us were working ruin upon poor James Griffin's planks, whilst the enemy's artillery dropped on us and around us a hail of missiles as various as they were far from contemptible. And when at length, carrying off our wounded, we fell back covered with glory and bruises, we had the satisfaction of knowing that James's planks could never again form a bridge for the Dutch, any more than they could form a building scaffold for their rightful owner.

The bridge was fairly kept and won, and the glorious victory must be duly celebrated. If the method of the celebration was not exactly historical, it was because the Vagabone, seeing that history had failed to rise to a great occasion, was determined to improve upon history.

"Dinny O'Friel," the Vagabone said, "you have done wan man's part, anyhow, as a warrior on the fiel' of battle this day; and now I want to see that ye'll act your part as a—a——"

"A statesman," I helped him.

"Ye've plunked your fut on it, like Phelimy caught the fluke," said he. "Yis, as a statesman; keepin' th' oul' man"—by which he irreverently signified his father—"in gab whilst we fire Athlone. When it's lingo that's in queskin it's bringin' mail to the mill to think to give you advice; only this, keep th' oul' man debatin' like the very dickens till ye hear three curlew-cries from the hill: then ye'll know Athlone 'ill be a burnin' past all redimption: and the farther ye are from th' oul man afther that, the farther ye'll be from danger. Them's all yer diractions."

Feeling not a little pride in the importance as well as in the risk of my embassy, I went direct to Toal's. I was in the nick of time: for, it being Saturday night, Toal had quit his work early, although 'twas yet only in the dusk, and had shaved and washed, and got on a collar and tie, meaning to idle like a gentleman whilst awaiting the advent of the day of rest. In another minute it is probable he would have been strolling out to take a well-earned mouthful of fresh air, strutting up the road, and patronizingly discoursing neighbours who could not afford the same luxurious leisure.

Billy Brogan was still upon the bench, and would be likely to remain on it till "the bordhers of mid-night"—which was usual for him on Saturday nights—as Tammas Haraghey, of Dhrumduff, who was already there, wanted his new brogues for Sunday.

"Youngsther," said Toal off-handedly, "what's the news without, the night?"

Things were critical, I saw at once, for Toal was carefully brushing three specks from his coat previous to sallying forth; so I was immediately alive to the necessity of barring him by something more than ordinarily strong. And good luck, which favoured me often, had on the night before placed me in possession of such.

"Big news entirely, Toal," I said.

"What? What is it?" said he hastily. Billy Brogan, too, despite his desperate hurry looked up from his work to read my face. And Tammas Haraghey, of Dhrumduff, and the neighbours there assembled, did likewise. For the thirst for news at Knockagar was always intense. All were now looking at me in attitude to drink in what I had to disclose.

I said: "My Uncle Donal sent me a message last night to Barney Mulrainy's, of Tullaghfin, for a fir-hatchet, and the *Bacach Fada** was there, and he was tellin' that the red-headed miller with two thumbs upon wan hand has come, and that he has a mill on the Sleibh Garbh water in the Rosses!"

"Ye don't tell me?" said Toal, flinging from him the whisk with which he had been brushing. And the others said "tchuk! tchuk!" in amazement.

Yet, though I did not half believe the surprising intelligence myself, I was truthfully repeating what I heard the *Bacach Fada* say.

Toal took a seat close beside me, and begged for further particulars. I had not many to give, except that the beggarman had said the miller was named

---

* The tall Beggarman.

Cnocher MacSweeny, and that there was no doubt of his existence, for he had been pointed out to him at the last fair of Doochary.

"Then," said Toal, "if that be so—and I see small raison to doubt it, or to question the *Bacach Fada's* veracity—it's the most amazin' bit of intelligence has come to the ears of livin' man in this present giniration. For it manes that we're likely to see in our day the most wondherful part of Sent Colm Cille's wondherful Prophecies comin' through, and the departure for iver of the Sassenach from our island."

"But," said the Widow's Pat, "there'll be awful happenin's!"

"With a gloryous endin'," said Toal.

"God sen' it soon and suddint," Billy Brogan said.

"As I rec'llect the Prophecy," Pat said, with a long-drawn face, "the last battles 'll be so thremendious that the mill wheel of the miller with two thumbs is to turn three times with human blood!"

"Ye have it corractly, Pathrick," Toal said. "And that'll be a chape price for liberty. And I mistake ye much if you, Pathrick, would begrudge yer heart's blood for Irelan'."

"Not me own—not me own—if I had oceans of it," Pat said. "But, Toal, it would go to the heart of me, cowl as I'd be in the green grave, to know that the country was disolate."

"Pathrick," said Toal solemnly, "there was a time when for all the miles and miles of green hills and valleys from Donegal town to Darry Walls, and from Sthrabane to Glenswilly, afther the Sassenach had done his work, the voice of a man or the low of a cow wasn't to be heard."

"It's so, Toal," Pat said resignedly.

"But afore the last of it all, this time, we're to see many wondhers, and suffer many hardships," Toal went on.

"The signs afore the end," Pat said.

"Yis, the signs afore the end," said Toal. "I have often toul' yous it was fast comin', and would be very likely to come in our time."

"Ye did, then, Toal. Ye did, then," the neighbors said.

"The Prophecies sayed all the wondherful happenin's were to occur in the reign of the thirteenth king and queen of haresy in England—which, as I worked it out, was bound to be this present reign."

"Ye've always sayed so, Toal," Pat said.

"Some of the signs has come in my day; the others 'ill soon come now."

"The seed," Toal went on, "was to wither from undher the sod, and the crops to be in mournin'—

which was the great potato blight of last year. A black pig puttin' fire and smoke from his nostrils is to run through Barnesmore gap: from the description Dinny Managhan the carter gives me of the railroad thrain which he seen the last time he was in Dublin, I'm of opinion that's what 'ill be the black pig. There'll be a period of awful disthress and daith, when the dead 'll be buried where they fall, and we'll not see the sun's face for thirteen weeks; but just afore that is to come a time of wonderful prosperity, when the face of the country 'ill smile, and a cow 'ill fetch the full of her horn of money; and a time after it when the three black cuts* is to be levied and gathered with steel hands. After the third cut has been lifted—which 'ill be in the early harvest, the corn 'ill fall and rot upon the ground, no man puttin' scythe or hook to it bekase each man tells his neighbour to keep the edge on his scythe to reap a harvest that hasn't been reaped for several hundred years——"

Toal's recital was, to the vexation of all of us, suddenly and rudely interrupted by Matt McCourt's bursting into the house with a bellow in his throat.

"Is it sittin' there ye are, claverin'?" he shouted in disdainful tones, "and your whole hill afire! and your bridge below lyin' in smithereens in the burn!

---

* Taxes.

and that young devil's imp beside ye, after bein' the main man undher your own son in wrackin' it, now keepin' ye gostherin' there, so the boys could burn the hill in paice. I'm just afther hearin' the whole story, and run up breathless to let ye know."

For the moment, I was paralyzed as much as Toal and the remainder of the circle. So absorbed had I become in Toal's words, that I quite forgot the burning of Athlone, and forgot to attend to the curlew-calls, which in all probability had been long since given.

When, in another moment, I realized my position, I resolved to take my leave—rather abruptly, I confess. In short I made a daring dash for the door, and so quickly did I execute the movement that I had it unlatched, half-open, and was almost through, when Toal's rough grasp fastened upon my collar; and, with very much reluctance on my part, I was withdrawn under his roof again.

"Billy Brogan," Toal said, in a voice whose severe calm struck terror to my soul, "reach me that sthrap hangin' on the nail beyont ye."

On that night I got my first flogging.

The hero of Athlone retired to Augherbeg, to exile.

CHAPTER XII.

ON THE ROAD TO THE FAIR.

As her uncle Pat had promised to bring Nuala to the great Harvest fair of Glenties, my imagination was fired, and I, too, longed to journey to a great fair, and see it for myself.

Though my Uncle Donal, as I have already said, gave me a great deal of freedom, that freedom was, still, only within the reasonable limits allowed for an irresponsible youngster's roaming. I had never been to a fair,—had never, in fact, sought to go to that which I believed to be so far beyond the wildest ambition of a youngster. Moreover, Uncle Donal himself seldom visited the fairs; he went when he had absolute business there, and quitted them for home as soon as that business was transacted.

The Harvest fair of Glenties was an event of vast importance, looked forward to with joyful anticipation for three-quarters of a year, and looked back upon with merry remembrance for the next quarter of a year, by all within a score of miles' radius.

At Nuala's solicitation and mine, the Widow's Pat approached my Uncle Donal in my interest. "I'm goin' to yock the little baste into the cart," Pat said to my uncle, "and dhraw little Yellow-Head to see the fair; and there's no reason why wee Dinny mightn't take a sate with us. The chile is naturally wishful for to see the seein's of life." And to my great joy, my Uncle Donal did not refuse. He said, "Yis, I'll not begrudge poor Dinny a day's enjoyment."

After a night during which the fever in my blood prevented me sleeping much, our little party took the road to Glenties at an early hour, I driving, Nuala seated by me, and Pat, under his broad-brimmed felt, walking alongside. I am sure the gladness in my heart added brightness to the morn; for, it seemed to me, that I had never beheld a morning so glorious. After timorously peeping for a while over the crest of the Croagh Ghorm hills the sun had come boldly up into a speckless sky, and now smiled benignly over the world, and every one that lived in the world. The leverocks were aloft raining their benisons upon the glad earth; and from the bushes by the wayside many birds chaunted their morning hymns. The purple-decked moors spread away, far and far, like flowered gigantic robes; and the scent of new hay filled the air.

"Eh, Nuala," I said. "Did ye ever see as grand a mornin'?"

"I think I never did," Nuala said. And she had a faraway look in her eyes as she absorbed the delights and the beauties with which the scene was so profusely strewn. And then she laughed at me when I said, "I do believe, Nuala, the sun and birds, and the moors, know this is the Harvest Fair of Glenties."

Pat looked upon both of us with gladness in his eyes, and he said half to himself, "God bliss yous, childre." We nodded and smiled upon Pat, and felt happier still.

The further we got along, the livelier and gayer did the scene become; for each little road, and lane, and *cosaidh** was bringing down from the moors and the hills its tribute of boys and girls all decked in their gayest, and of men and women in their whitest and neatest—some walking, some riding on saddle or pillion—and many driving with them kine that lowed for the harsh hills they were leaving; though the more thoughtless calves frisked as if (I pointed out to Pat) even they felt the excitement of the Harvest Fair of Glenties in their blood.

---

* Cassey—footway.

The throng was thickening each succeeding mile we went; every one was glad, and every one was joyous. Loud and cheery greetings were shouted, and joke and banter and chaff was passed and bandied. All hearts were merry, and all tongues were free, and in all eyes danced the brightness of the morn.

"Small wondher they're gay-hearted, the craitures," Pat said. "They've lost many a baid of sweat for a month back, to earn this wan idle day for themselves, and many's the wan of them has scraped hard for a shillin' to help the gaiety of it."

More than the bright ribbons of the girls and the highly greased boots of the boys, what took Nuala's fancy was the picture of the mountain man and his wife and pony. Over a moor or rough road; from the hearts of the hills they came—the little squat pony as rough and shaggy as the shaggiest bit of his native heath, his homespun-clad, knee-breeched owner, as wiry looking and hardy as the straw-saddled, straw-bridled animal he bestrode, and the blue-cloaked, white-capped, *bean-an-tighe** pillion-seated upon the animal's haunches, insuring her seat by circling with one arm the waist of him who sat in front and guided the destinies of the party. The *bean-an-tighe* carried in her free hand a linen handkerchief, and with it mopped occasionally a grave brow—grave, because there

* Housewife.

rested on her the care of a lord, light-headed on such a day, and the care of all that lord's cares—which were sure to be shaken to her ere the day was half over.

"Be the boots," said Pat, "if here isn't the Masther an' Ellen Burns a-horseback, too!" And as Nuala and myself suddenly turned around, a cheer from the Masther greeted us, as he cantered up and slacked speed at our side. Nuala's eyes were dancing, and she clapped her hands and cheered in return; to which the Masther doffed as statelily as any knight of yore. And Ellen, glancing around him, from the pillion-seat behind, waved her handkerchief to myself and Nuala.

"Salutation to thee, Yellow Head!" the Masther said to Nuala. "And to thee, Dionysius!—A salubrious morning, Patrick!—The prancing steed that you observe with not incurious look, I obtained from Bartholomew Martin of the Diminutive Plateau—more familiar to your ears perhaps, Patrick, under the denomination of Bartley Martin of the Alt Beag. Bartholomew graciously extended to me the favour, for this long-anticipated day. And my valued friend Fair Eleanor——" he waved his hand backwards—"deigned to honour the noble quadruped and myself. So, gaily and merrily, we go to the Fair."

Then he put a hand into his pocket and drew out

a purse. It was not very fat, in sooth. Yet, smiling benevolently, he took out four pennies singly, and gracefully tossed them into Nuala's lap. "On such a day," he said, "lack not for gold and silver whilst Bartholomew Whorisky bears a money-bag. This humble donation apportion equitably betwixt thy Ladyship and Dionysius."

Two whole pennies each! I almost crowed with delight. Three pennies I was now, for the first time in my life, possessed of—having had a penny from my Uncle Donal. I glanced up at Ellen; and she was beaming upon me, as much gladdened by my delight as I was by my undreamt-of riches.

"Dinny!" she said, shaking at me a roguish finger. "Mind, I'm the only girl you're to spend money on, the day."

"Never fear, Ellen, but I'll mind that," I said with a serious earnestness that made Ellen smile lovingly, and the Masther laughed outright.

"Dionysius, my lad," he said, "I warn you that as I am for this day in possession of this fickle maiden, by paternal assignment, I shall tolerate no rival. Beware!"

Ellen smiled again and kissed back her hand to me, as they cantered off. I, looking longingly after, strove to urge our donkey to a hotter pace, but Pat ran forward, and laying hold of the reins, checked the animal's hastening progress.

We soon, to our delight, came up with Billy Brogan, who was resting on the ditch a creel of brogues, that in straw arm-ropes he had been carrying on his back all the way from home.

"Thank God yous have come along," Billy said, "for the heart of me's nigh bruck under such a load of brogues in the mornin'. Nothin' would do Toal but he'd fetch a venture of them to the fair—sweet good luck to both him and them!"

Pat had the creel of brogues deposited in the bed of the cart very soon, and the troubled look was fast leaving Billy's brow, as he stepped lightly alongside.

Nuala, shaking her curls at Billy, assured him that he was looking elegant this morning, to which compliment Billy blushed and smiled a self-conscious smile, and he said, "I'll buy you the nicest penny ribbon in the fair, Nuala."

Nuala said, "Thank ye ever so much, Billy; and I'll be very proud of it. But what about Ellen Burns, Billy?" and she smiled mischievously.

Billy looked grave instantly. He came close up alongside Nuala, and drawing from the inside pocket of his waistcoat a linen handkerchief, he exhibited to her a corner of it into which was knotted a circular object: "Do ye know what that is, Nuala?" he said.

Nuala said, "That's the size of a tenpenny."*

"And that's what it is," said Billy; and he added earnestly, "I saved that tenpenny all for Ellen, and as far as it goes upon her she'll not want for fairlies, I give ye my word."

"Poor Billy!" Nuala exclaimed in alarm, "and what'll ye do for yourself?"

"Is it me?" Billy said, proudly. "Why, afther that, I've more money nor† ye could wag a stick at. I've been gatherin' and scrapin' for ten weeks for this day." And he hereupon exhibited another corner of the handkerchief which knotted-in a cylindrical bulk that from its dimensions suggested nine or ten copper pennies. And Billy smiled when he saw the alarm hereupon subside from Nuala's countenance. When he replaced his treasure, and buttoned it up, he patted Nuala upon the head affectionately.

I had been looking at and listening to all this, with just the faintest shade of discontent upon my mind. And I now said, "I am going to buy Ellen Burns the best ribbon she can pick for tuppence."

Billy replied, without a trace of jealousy, "Throth, and for tuppence ye'll get the gran'est ribbon that's to be had for love or money, atween here and

---

* Tenpenny silver pieces were then current in Ireland.

† Than.

Amerikay." Billy, for a moment, fingered his waistcoat about the region whereunder his hoard of coppers lay. Then he said, "I'll give ye a penny in the fair meself, Dinny, me boy."

I replied instantly, "Thanky, Billy Brogan, very kindly. But I've more money nor I know what to do with"—untruthfully; but I felt above accepting a favour from a rival. I confess my conscience stung me just a little, when Nuala turned solemn eyes upon me. But I refused to meet her gaze.

I said to Billy, "Ye saw Ellen passin', a-horse-back with the Masther?"

"I did, I did. May Goodness bliss her!" Billy replied.

"Don't ye think," I said, regretfully, "that the Masther 'll spend a deal of money on her?"

"Och, the Masther!" Billy said, lightly. "He's a rag on every bush; there'll not be six girls in the fair he'll not be putting the comether on." Which gave me secret satisfaction.

Nuala said, "Do you know, Billy, that Dinny here says he'll marry Ellen Burns."

Billy gave me a kind, but amused look, which hurt me, for I interpreted it without difficulty. And I said warmly, "Billy Brogan, I'll be big before long—as big as you."

"Oh, ye will, Dinny. Sure, I know ye will," he said hastily.

"And there's Nuala, and she's scarce as big as me; and she's only a woman; and she means to marry the Masther," I said.

Nuala looked reflective for a moment. And then she said, "I don't know now, Dinny—I'm afraid the Masther would sooner have Ellen. And I know Ellen likes him, for I've seen her blush often and often when he's come into her father's."

Though Nuala's words more than half-hurt myself, my attention was arrested by their effect upon Billy. He fell suddenly silent, and looked downcast. After a little time, during which no word was spoken, he abruptly said, "I don't believe it, Nuala Gildea! I mane to say," he added hurriedly, "that ye've entirely mistuk it. And if Ellen did blush, sure anyhow the blushes on her come and go like an aiddy wind. And I've seen her blush when meself walked into her father's." Billy was evidently trying hard to believe this. "And I'm sure she smiles on me like an April sun wheniver I go in," he said, with a tone of something like defiance.

"I know she does," little Nuala said softly. "She smiles very kindly on ye surely, and seems always delighted to see ye."

"And there ye are!" Billy said, conclusively. "Besides," he added, gratuitously, "I only wish, Nuala, you'd seen the shilute and the smile she gave me as she rode past this mornin' and me bent two double inunder the creel of brogues was on me back!"

I had to confess to myself that in the Masther and Billy Brogan I had two serious rivals for Ellen's much-coveted favour.

Billy's whistling in the dark so far restored his serenity that he was enabled to strike up a fugitive verse:

"It was on a summer's morning in the fragrant month of
May,
Down by the banks of Claudy I carelessly did stray;
I overheard a fee-male disthressfully complain
All for her absent lover that ploughed the ragin' main.

"I advanced my steps unto her, and give her a surprise,
I own she didn't know me, I being in disguise;
And I says, my fairest creature, your grace I do adore
Come share with me the miserie so loudly you deplore."

Pat was coming along behind, chatting with one of the bands of fair-goers that were very thick upon the road now we were near Glenties.

CHAPTER XIII.

AT THE BIG HARVEST FAIR OF THE GLENTIES.

THE street of Glenties, and the gateways off it, and all vacant spaces by it, were crammed with people and cattle, and carts, and tents, and apple-stands; and the houses were thronged to the doors, and to the windows, out of which hundreds were leaning watching the great gay, surging crowd on the street below. The moving, and talking, and shouting, and crying of the thousands that hid the street, filled my ears with one continuous roar, that for a while awed and daunted me, who had never before heard anything remotely approaching it. But the—as it seemed to me—seething mass of people who struggled for passage wheresoever they wished to move, had fascination for me, and I was standing in wonder, looking at the puzzling sight, when a volley of ear-piercing whistles was fired behind me, the ground seemed to tremble, and I was snatched away to the side of the road just in time to escape being trampled to death by a solid herd of great, long-horned bullocks that were being whacked violently by many drivers, with ash-plants, and pressed and driven at a rattling speed right up the centre of the crowd-jammed street. And, thickly packed as the immense crowd had stood, they divided like water at a ship's prow, and tumbled over one another, to left and to right, over throwing not only angry men and screaming women, but also *dilisc* stands and apple stalls, carts of fish and crockery-ware, and "standings" of fairlies; which deepened in me the strange impression with which I had come to look, for the first time in my life, on such a mass of humanity congregated for business and pleasure.

Pat guided Nuala and myself down the street, forcing a way for himself with one shoulder which he used wedge-like. We stood to gaze at all the different stands and stalls that were ranged along both sides of the way. And we observed the drinking tents, and the *Spailin* tents, where potatoes and fish and mutton were boiled, and served up to hasty, hungry customers. He took us to the house of a friend of his own, Mrs. McCue, where all three of us enjoyed a hearty meal, with flannel bread and oat bread well buttered—for the long morning drive had given us a hearty appetite. After such a satisfying meal, Nuala and I confessed to each other that we felt much better fit for the delights of the fair.

Out into it we wandered (after much sage advice from her uncle Pat, who was now going by himself to attend to business), and through it where we list. We saw, and were proud to be smiled upon by, many Knockagar folk. Corney Higarty whom we found going through the fair, and twirling his blackthorn, like the gentleman of leisure he was, took us to an apple-stand, and stuffed our pockets with that coveted fruit. In a drinking tent into which we looked curiously, we discover John Burns and Toal a-Gallagher arguing Scripture across the board with (to us) strange opponents—men, who,—I knew by their gravely sage expression—must have been, in their own country, oracles scarcely less noted than were John and Toal in ours.

Let Nuala wish to go where she might, I always strove to drag her wherever a ballad-singer's shrill tones gathered an eagerly attentive crowd; as the day wore on, and the more serious business of the fair slackened, the number of ballad-singers and the proportions of their audience increased. Intent as I had been upon husbanding my money, I spent my one spare penny almost before I knew, upon the purchase of two ballads—beautiful ballads they seemed to me, for one of them roused the enthusiasm of the audience to a high pitch, and the other drew their tears. The former, like most of the ballads in the fair, was, of course, about Dan:

"O'Connell our hero he planted the tree,
Saying 'Irishmen, whack away! die or be free.'"

though the ballad-singer gave it in his own style.

"O'Connell orairo ye planted a three
Sayin' 'Irishmen, whackaway! die and be free.'"

The second ballad was the very mournful one of the murder of young Rosie Connolly—or as the ballad had it, Rosie Connollie:

"It was on a Monday morning my Rosie I did meet,
With a bottle of cherry brandy to give my Rose a treat;
With a bottle of cherry brandy inunder an ivy tree,
It's there I ended the days of Rosie Connollie."

"Young Rosie Connollie loved me, dear as she loved her life,
Full sore I did repent I made her not my wife.
Full sore I did repent it upon the gallows-tree
That e'er I ended the days of young Rosie Connollie."

And when I had expended my penny upon these, it gave me a pang that I could not purchase a ballad which, bawled out at another part of the street, seized hold of my fancy, a "Lament for Thaidy":

"Now who will win the harvest? and who will mow the hay?
And who is to do anything? since Thaidy's gone away."

And another, which I equally craved for:

" Attention pay both young and old
Unto these lines I do unfold,
The deeds of brave Napoleon, sure, I'm going for to relate;
How, many years most manfullie
He sthruggled hard for libertie—
A most immortial hairo was Napoleon Boneypart."

An old gray man—old in years only; by no means so in spirit—who had evidently been a contemporary of the great and idolised Boneypart, by the free use of his blackthorn staff cleared, and kept clear, a circular space around the singer, constituting himself patron of Napoleon's memory. An immense crowd surged around the singer, and with every sign of intense enthusiasm strained their ears to catch every syllable of the praises of the immortal hero. And, when the singer had finished, the gray-headed patron of Napoleon helped him to distribute the ballads to the eager multitude, and to take in the halfpennies therefor. "Buy them up! Buy them up! Buy them up!" he cried, waving the blackthorn over his head the while, "for Irelan's thruest frien' was the immortial Boneyparty." But, to the crowd, which crushed and pushed to possess the ballad, both the encouragement and the information were foolishly superfluous.

Nuala and I made our way out betwixt the legs of the surging mass. And the regret I felt then was a very trifle compared with my vexation an hour later, when I discovered something which, though far more exciting still, I was unable to procure, because of the same unfortunate lack of funds. This was a leaflet, which, for a penny, an old man was steadily serving out to the crowd as fast as he could. By the old man's side stood a tall pole exhibiting a great placard which, in large ill-formed letters, announced to all whom it might concern, that,

THE WHOLE SOLE AND TRUE ACCOUNT OF THE COMBAT

BETWEEN FATHER DEVENNY AND THE DEVIL

FOR THE SOWL OF BRIANY DOHERTY,

was there, to be purchased for one penny. One-half the large placard was taken up by a rude picture which intended to show Briany on his death-bed extending appealing arms to Father Devenny upon his right, while the Devil known by his tail, hoof, and streak of red coming out of his mouth, to the left was striving to raise the dying man on his shoulders. It was now I repented the foolish jealousy that had prompted me to scout Billy Brogan's kind promise of a penny.

At a standing of fairlies, Nuala and myself were surprised by the Masther and Ellen, who had come forward to patronize the goods displayed. The Masther expressed himself as "enchanted to encounter both, for I am desirous of doing myself the delight of speculating for your behoof, in some of the multifarious attractions here displayed."

"Dinny, what have you done with all your money?" Ellen asked me, as she stroked my cheek.

"I've bought grand ballads with some of it," I said. "And I've kept some to buy a ribbon for you."

Nuala said, "He left out a penny on ballads, and there was others he wanted to buy bad; only he wouldn't, because he was keepin' the other tuppence to buy your ribbon."

I looked a resentful look at Nuala. But Ellen stooped, and kissed me on the cheek, which, done in the open fair, made me blush deeply.

I said, "Ellen, I want you to choose a ribbon now."

Ellen looked me in the eye with a soft look; then pressed my head between both her hands for a little while.

"Dinny," she said, "you're my wee sweetheart." Here I blushed again, and a pleasurable tingle sped through my veins—"A dear, good, wee sweetheart," she said. "I cannot take your ribbon,

Dinny; you must spend the tuppence on yourself and on Nuala. And here too's another penny, take from me, to buy more ballads."

I drew myself away vexedly from the proffered penny. "No," I said, with decision. "I want to buy you a tuppenny ribbon," I added; "won't ye pick one?"

"Oh, no, no, no, dear Dinny, no," she said. "I couldn't think of taking away your tuppence from ye. Won't you take this penny to buy ballads?"

I only pushed her hand away, and did not speak for vexation. The Masther now engaged her attention, for he had been purchasing lavishly for her. I saw him give her two ribbons that cost him sixpence each, and a brooch that cost him a shilling, and several other knick-knacks. Then, for Nuala, he bought a necklace, and a fancy pen.

"And what does friend Dionysius choose?" he then inquired.

"Nothing, I thank you," I said, turning away.

But he laid a hand on my shoulder, and turned me again. "Dionysius," he said, "some souvenir of your first fair, have from me."

"Thank you, Masther, no," I said, keeping my face away.

"A delectable book is proffered to me for three paltry pence—'The Irish Rogues and Rapparees, videlicet.'"

I said, sullenly: "Ye are too good, Masther, and I've taken too much from ye," and turned away. I meant and felt the latter—for the twopence which I had had from him was burning my hand. I was still master of just enough good taste not to tender the money back to him.

Ellen's attention was, during this time, taken up with a girl friend whom she had met at the standing. And afterwards, when my judgment was cooler, I confessed to myself that I knew she was not aware of the soreness of feeling her refusal of my proposed gift had caused me.

As we proceeded through the fair Nuala upbraided me for my stubbornness and ill-temper. I bore all she said with patience. I took her to another fairlie-standing, and bought for my twopence a puce ribbon for her, and a pipe for my Uncle Donal—each of which cost a penny. Nuala took the ribbon gladly, showing the pleasure in her eye, which, in turn, pleased me much, and I glowed with the pride of a great benefactor.

Brushing down her yellow hair with my hand, I said, in the tone of one who has made a pleasant discovery, "Nuala, you are very good! I was afraid you might hurt me, too, by refusin' the ribbon bekase I didn't make offer of it to you till I found I had no other use for the money."

Nuala was leaning one hand on my shoulder. She said, looking into my eyes: "Dinny, ye had plenty of other use for the money. Ye could have bought ballads with it—which ye wanted badly to do. And ye could have bought many and many another thing. I wouldn't do such an ugly thing as to refuse it—because I knew that ye railly wish it to me. It was ever so good of ye, Dinny, and I'm ever so glad to get such a lovely ribbon; and I'll always keep it, Dinny, and it'll mind me of you and of this lovely day."

I looked back into Nuala's serious eyes, and I said to myself, "God bless ye, Nuala!" Then I spoke aloud, saying tentatively, "Ach, Nuala, sure that wee rag of ribbon is nothin' to what the Masther give ye?"

"The Masther was very, very good—he's always good to me—and his gifts is very handsome," looking at them. "But yours is better, Dinny, and pleasanter to me, because ye left out your last penny on it."

I wished to be convinced; and now I was almost happy. I looked fondly on Nuala, and stroked her yellow hair again; and I said: "There's a whole lot of goodness in your wee heart, Nuala, that I never thought of." Whereat Nuala looked pleased —pleased, I know, that I was pleased.

We listened to the droll rants of the apple-sellers, who stood upon their stands, and canted out their apples in ha'pennyworths, singing out, "Rowl up! Rowl up! Rowl up! for another of the big ha'porth's. We bought them dear, and we'll sell them chaip; and these niver grew in a graveyard. There's two for Rosie, two for Micky, two for Jinny, Paddy, and Kitty, two for your wife, and wan to carry ye home—Houl' over your basket, ma'am, or your bonnet—Soul' again! Soul' again! to a Lady in her own right with ten hundherd a year, her choice of turf-stacks to stale from, and a tailyor for a likely son-in-law. God bliss ye, ma'am, and may ye live till I cut yer throat, and three days afther. Rowl up! Rowl up! Rowl up! for another of the big ha'porths!"

But Nuala thought she discerned her uncle Pat's peculiarly broad-brimmed felt in the centre of a crowd, and when, by squeezing between people's legs, I pioneered her within, we found her uncle there, attending to a man who concealed a pea under one of three thimbles upon a board, shuffled the thimbles, and offered to bet any sum, from a shilling to a pound, that no one present could locate the pea-thimble. I was very much excited, and Nuala likewise, when Pat took a well-shabbed leathern purse from an inside vest pocket, chose a tenpenny therefrom, and laid it on the board with trembling fingers. I knew well how very much a tenpenny meant to poor Pat. Consequently I was in as great trepidation as he. The gambler, after vainly endeavouring to induce Pat to increase the bet, covered the tenpenny with another, and held a protecting hand over both whilst he ordered Pat to "choose the thimble and win a fortune." Though Pat, in common with all of the now highly excited ones around was quite certain of the thimble underneath which the pea had been put, he hesitated a little—naturally enough, considering the sum at hazard. I impulsively placed my ash stick across the board and touched the thimble, saying, "That's it, Pat." Then the gambler raised loud and indignant protest to the public at large against the unfair advantage taken of him, and earnestly pleaded to be allowed to shuffle the thimbles again —which Pat and the public and I would not permit. So the gambler had to content himself with the indignant remonstrance that we were "fifty-five to one, combined to rob an orphant, and deprive him of an honest means of livelihood," whilst Pat, with now hasty movements, reached for the thimble and lifted it, discovering—no pea!

Pat was downcast. Nuala and I were downcast. All were dismayed, except the gambler, who, with undue haste, pocketed the two silver pieces, and further solaced himself with the spoken reflection that "Providence ever and always protects the orphant."

"But we'll give you another chance to win back your money. Faint heart never won fortune. There it goes again—in there. Now a quick eye and an open purse—them's all ye want and all ye need to win fame and name, and more besides, at this board, which is patronized by born ladies and bred jintlemen, and the crowned heads of Europe, Asia, Isaac, and Jacob. To do all things fair, square, and above board is our motive; for although we're poor we are not dishonest, and pay all winnin's in goold; exceptin' large sums, for which we give a cheque upon Taigy Raigan's turf-bank. And now, again, sir, I'll give ye any bait, from one shillin' to the Bank of Ireland, that ye don't find the pea."

The mere gambling instinct was temporarily killed in Pat; but an eager desire to regain his own was strong in him. After a good deal of hesitation, he unclasped the purse again, and, drawing out another tenpenny, placed it on the board, where it was quickly covered by the gambler. He laid his hand, then, upon the very thimble—none of us could be mistaken this time—under which the pea had been placed, and lifted it. To the consternation of all, there was no pea!

I looked upon poor Pat as a man ruined for life. I saw Nuala look at him, and the tears well in her blue eyes. There was something biting painfully in my bosom, which instantly made me feel as I had never felt in my life before—ferocious. I saw the fellow's hand was on the board, sweeping the tenpennies therefrom, and, without an instant's hesitation, I swung my ashplant aloft, regardless of the heads of those who stood behind me, and with a savage delight I brought it down swoop upon, unfortunately—for I could not aim well because of a mist that was on my eyes—only the points of his fingers. But it made him howl with pain. I swung my weapon again for a more effective blow, but it would not come down. It was held in the air, and a rough grasp was at the same time laid on my shoulder, which rude interference allowed the gambler (to my bitterness of spirit) time to pocket the tenpennies.

"In the name of Napoleon Boneyparty, sure it isn't Dinny O'Friel rowin'?"

It was Corney Higarty who spoke, and Corney Higarty who held me. I glared at him and almost howled, "Corney Higarty, let go of me or I'll kick ye. This scoundrel is afther chaitin' Pat of two tenpennies."

"Be the thimbles? Oh, indeed," said Corney, not much disconcerted by my strange manner. "I understan' a thing or two about the honesty of that little game." And, turning me aside with a firm hand, he sprang forward and got hold of the gambler by the shirt-neck, shaking him till I thought I heard the bones rattle. "Turn out your dishonest gains," Corney thundered, "and hand them back to their rightful owner this instant. Or if ye don't, be the powdhers o' war I'll shake the sowl-case clean out o' ye!" But the terrified gambler needed not any further demonstration of Corney's intentions. As hastily as he could, he unpocketed two tenpennies and passed them toward Pat, who was standing by, dumbfounded at such unexpected and so forceful championing of his cause: and who, moreover, hesitated now about accepting the money.

"Take it, ye gommeral Pat!" shouted Corney, who still held a detaining hand on the gambler's shirt-neck. "Take it! I know this game afore; and the money was taken from ye mainer, and more barefacedly dishonest, than if it had 'a' been picked out of your pocket unknownst."

Pat took the money. Corney gave the orphan's bones a final rattle; and then conducted all of us off till he would treat us to refreshments. As we went, the now rejoicing Pat smiled upon me a grateful smile, and Nuala enclasped my arm in both of hers, and clung to it, looking up into my face with fond gratitude. Corney slapped me on the back, and said, " He's a hairo, is Dinny."

And as I strutted down the fair I felt that I was a hero.

CHAPTER XIV.

WHEN BILLY'S TEMPER WAS BRUCK

I WOULD not accept the penny Pat pressed upon me, because I felt it was not consonant with the character of a hero. But after another refreshing meal in Mrs. McCue's, at Corney's expense this time, Nuala and I accepted the loads of apples which Pat and Corney bought for us.

We came upon our friend Billy measuring brogues to customers' feet in a gateway, where he had taken his stand. The brogues were being rapidly sold out at half-a-crown each; one brogue to this customer, two brogues to that, and perhaps three to the other. For the brogues being conveniently made upon the same last, any of them fitted a right foot or a left, as the wearer wished or wanted it.

Billy was not courteous to his customers. He was in rank ill-humour—to our surprise.

"If ye don't like it, ma'am, ye can laive it," he

was saying to a woman anent a brogue which she held in her hand, "and it doesn't make a thraneen of differ to me, which ye do."

"The brogue's like your temper—it's too short for me," the woman replied tartly.

"If we had 'a' had your tongue for a last, ma'am, the mistake wouldn't happened," Billy said drily.

The woman looked narrowly at him and asked:

"Did they put ye to sleep on nettles las' night?"

"If ye're goin' to buy the brogue, buy it; if ye're not, ma'am, kindly move off, for I prefer your room to your company."

"Will ye take two-and-thruppence for it, Shugar-tongue?"

"I'll not take two-and-fippence-ha'penny for it, Misthress Skinflint," said Billy, decisively.

The woman contemptuously tossed the brogue into the creel again, gave Billy a withering look, and moving off, said:

"I'd advise ye, next time ye come to the fair of Glenties, to bring a better quality of both manners and brogues."

Billy would give a parting shot:

"There's some," he said caustically, "has but the wan quality of manners to choose from—and them's the divil's own manners."

She turned round. "I might 'a' supposed as much," she said, "and I'm sorry for ye."

Billy's compliment was so accurately turned upon himself that he was struck silent, whilst the woman walked off with the honors of war.

I said to Billy, as soon as he had time to notice us, that there was surely something the matter with him.

"Throth, Dinny, there is," he said. "If there wasn't do you think I'd be afther evenin' my wit to that varago of a woman?"

He had his creel almost empty of brogues. He turned it on its side, thus making a seat for himself. He shared the seat with Nuala, and he related to me how, having proposed to Ellen Burns to spend the tenpenny upon her, she would not hear of it. This, he said, was the cause of his ill-humor. "Isn't it, or not cause sufficient?" he added bitterly.

So, in Billy I had a companion in misfortune, which was, in some measure, a relief to me. I told him how seriously Ellen had displeased and offended me in like manner, and of the presents she had accepted from the Masther. Billy remained silent and thoughtful for a while, and then he said, half to himself:

"Ay, ay! I thought so. I thought as much— Well," he added with a sigh of desperation, "your life's a blank to ye now, Billy Brogan. So ye may as well enjoy it. A short life and a merry wan."

Young as I was, it struck me there was something illogical about Billy's soliloquy. He arose off the seat, gently moved Nuala also, and turned up the creel again, singing out to the passers-by, "Rowl up! Rowl up! and buy chape brogues for yourselves and your wives and grown up childhre. It's the chance of a lifetime to get the best brogues ever was turned off a last for half-a-crown apiece. And anywan too poor, too mane, or too niggardly to pay that much won't be turned away barefutted if they offer me even two-and-six. Rowl up! Rowl up! There's only thirteen remainin' to clear me out; and upon my varacity as a shoemaker if yous don't buy them up in purty quick time, I'll clear the creel meself, and pelt yous out of the fair with them. Rowl up! Rowl up!"

Bad though Billy's temper undoubtedly was just then, he paused from railing at the public to press a penny each on myself and Nuala. I had too much sympathy for him to refuse my penny, and I knew by the look in Nuala's eye, that she took his penny for a like reason.

"Nuala," he said gently as he closed her hand on the penny, "ye're the purtiest *cailín* walks the fair this day—barrin' wan," he added with a sad, reflective shake of the head, "barrin' wan."

About half an hour later we met Billy again. He was passing a drinking tent, walking with a swagger, and swinging a blackthorn. The hat was set on his head with a devil-may-care poise, there was a strange light in his eye, and he was singing a mournful song to a ranting air—

> "And when ye hear my ditty,
> 'Twill move yer heart to pity,
> Of a murther near our city,
> At a place called Ireland's Eye.
> Tee rum tum addity O!"

In fact Nuala and I saw to our sorrow that Billy had been drowning his grief since we parted with him.

"Yellow-head, me jewel! how are ye?" he cried out. "And Dinny, me lad, how's every rib in ye? Meself's as merry as a mouse in a mill. Whoop! Hurroo!" waving his stick aloft. "In all me born days I niver seen a fair as full of fun. Dinny, *a gradh*, why don't ye enjoy yourself? What did your stick grow for? Hurroo! Hoogh! Wherever ye see a head hit it!" And to my affright, he brought his blackthorn whack down upon the shape of a head where it showed through the tent-cloth. There was instantly uproar within; from the tent came a rush of men brandishing sticks aloft; and they had surrounded Billy in another moment. In alarm Nuala clung to me. I half closed my eyes, unwilling to see poor Billy felled, and unable to save him. But Billy's stick dropped; and all the sticks dropped.

"In the name of wonder, Billy Brogan, ye don't mane to say it was you sthruck me?" It was only then I observed that the leader in the rush was Toal, whose half-castor bore an irretrievable dinge. And Owen-a-Slaivin and John Burns and big Matthew McCourt were Toal's henchmen in the sally. Toal's voice was filled with fraternal reproach.

"I didn't know it was you, Toal,"—Billy's eyes were on the ground, but there was a perverse doggedness in his tone. "I did not know, Toal, it was you;" raising his eyes, and infusing more ring into his tone, "but as I've done it, I've done it, and may the divil take me if I care!" And he was now gripping his blackthorn tightly again and looking from Toal to his henchmen with a dauntless defiance that made me almost feel proud of him.

Toal looked fixedly at Billy for a few moments, and then sadly and slowly shook his head.

"I don't care, Toal—I don't care, Toal," Billy said in reply to Toal's head-shake. "I'm not the mane-spirited man for to go and rue anything I do. Besides," he added, as a bright idea flashed upon him, "you've been my masther for three years and seven months, and in all of that time I've never given ye a crack. So," and he here flourished the stick overhead, "it's little enough that I'd get the pleasure of wan at ye now—This is the Harwist Fair of Glenties! Whoop! Hoogh! Hurroo!" And but that Owen-a-Slaivin, and John, and Matthew, flung themselves on Billy, and, after a struggle, wrenched from him the stick, Toal's head would have come in for further favours.

Toal's superior self-esteem was very much outraged. He turned and walked into the tent again in dignified silence. Sending Billy away weaponless and a bit downcast, Toal's henchmen followed him within, where, I had little doubt, they encouraged him to seek solace in a tumbler of poteen, whilst they remedied the dinge in his Sunday hat, which (I knew well) they could not do for the unfortunate dinge in his dignity.

Far better it would have been, I believe, had they left his stick with Billy. As it developed afterwards, he wandered down the fair, disconsolate and crestfallen, till he reached Maura Managhan's stocking stall. At sight of Maura's wares his eye lit up and his gladness of heart returned. Fortunately for him Maura, good woman, had her attention temporarily attracted elsewhere whilst he deliberately selected the longest and strongest stocking on the stand. He bore it off joyously, and, further on, picked up a stone of ten pounds weight, which he dropped into it. Then it was not very many minutes later till the word, borne by a breathless messenger, was carried to our part of the fair that Billy Brogan was cleaning out the fair with a stone in a stocking!

Seeing Toal and his three comrades making a dash down the street, I placed Nuala in good hands and ran also. We heard particularly great noise, and saw signs of particularly great commotion at a point far down; and as we with some difficulty neared it, we observed a forest of blackthorns swaying high in the air.

"Upon my soul," said Owen-a-Slaivin, "Billy 'll be gettin' all the fun he wants."

Toal groaned, saying "He's a parvarse boy, is William."

We found Corney Higarty and Pat there before us, pleading (in vain) with Billy, from a safe distance. Billy, with the big stone in the foot of the stocking, was using a long and effective weapon for cleaning out the fair. He had hold of the stocking by the head, had taken one turn of it over his hand for greater security, and was steadily marching onwards swinging his weapon at arm's length, and driving before him a reluctant and dense mass of men, who angrily waved their blackthorns in air, and strove to encourage one another to stand their ground and close with Billy—but in vain. We were compelled to back, back, back steadily with the rest of the great crowd.

"Billy! Billy! Billy! for God's sake what's wrong with ye? Give over with your antics like a daicent boy," Corney Higarty called to him.

"Hoop! Hoogh! Hurroo!" Billy replied, swinging the stocking more forcibly than ever. "This is the Harwist Fair of Glenties, Corney. I'm out for fun, and fun I'll have. A short life and a merry wan for me. Corney, me lad, will ye do me the favour of standin' your ground till I get the pleasure of wan crack at ye? Hoogh! Hoogh! Hoop! Hurroo!"

Corney did not see his way to afford Billy the coveted pleasure. But at this moment, Maura Managhan, to whom had been carried news of her pilfered stocking and of the then whereabouts and doings of the pilferer, threw the angry crowd to left and right—for Maura was a lusty woman and powerful of muscle—as she forced her way through. Nor did she for one moment hesitate when she reached the limit of security as defined by the crowd's inner edge. She sprang straight at Billy, ducking her head to permit the swing of his weapon free passage above. Billy staggered back half a pace at the unexpectedness and audacity of the charge; and ere he recovered himself, Maura, taking him by the neckcloth with one hand, held him rigidly while she swiped him on the side of the head with the other. In his endeavour to back away from her his heel tripped and he fell—Maura's grip upon his neckcloth letting him down somewhat easier, though, than otherwise would have been the case. Maura then snatched from his slackened grasp the stocking which she sought; and after reviling him, where he lay helpless, and informing him that he might well be proud of himself for "thryin' to take a poor woman's bite out of her mouth," emptied the stone upon him, gave him a reminder in the form of a slap across the face with the hosiery, and departed grumbling.

The instant Maura turned from him there arose among the crowd angry cries for reprisals upon him; but, headed by the valiant Corney, the Knockagar men rushed in, brandishing their sticks, and after very few minutes' brisk fighting compelled the crowd to a sullen retreat.

When Billy, after due deliberation, arose to his feet, the spirit had completely ebbed out of him. Toal said naught, only cast upon him a sorrowfully reproachful glance—which was lost on him, for his head hung, weighted with the disgrace of ignominious defeat at the hands of a woman!

I knew well Corney craved to rebuke him, but

was restrained by chivalrous ideas. Pat, full of sympathy, took him under his wing, and quitted him not until he saw him at home, safely and soberly in Knockagar that night.

CHAPTER XV.

THE OUTCAST WREN.

ON that painful day on which I had killed the poor leverock in Glenboran, I, in bitterness of spirit, vowed to myself that I would never again run the risk of wantonly injuring one of God's birds. And afterwards every time I visited the house of the Widow's Pat, I confirmed me in my resolve, for in the few square yards of flower garden which Pat and Nuala cultivated in front of the cabin, a standing stone that marked the grave of the leverock, forced itself painfully on my attention. Nuala had got her uncle to help her inter the body of the poor, dead songbird lovingly, had erected a little flag above it, and grown flowers upon the grave.

As soon as she permitted me to speak to her after the crime, I had told Nuala my resolve and mollified her somewhat. And henceforward, by force of little

Nuala's example, I had a more tender and loving interest in all the birds; and I was much more careful to conceal my nest from all except Nuala, who was now my usual companion on bird-nesting expeditions. I had presented to her a pair of young wild pigeons from the larch tree in Eamon's grove, and, despite the almost insuperable difficulty of taming them, she had in a great measure succeeded, and had raised from them many further pairs, which were still further divorced from wild life and the woods. For their accommodation Corney Higarty had constructed and presented Nuala with an elegant dovecote, of which when it hung on his gable her uncle Pat was not less proud than herself. The Master, too, was much pleased with it, and delighted in referring to it, in casual conversation, as "Patrick's Aviary." In time the pigeons became so fond of the gentle Nuala that they would, to the wonder and delight of all Knockagar, come at her call and light upon her head, her shoulders and her hands.

"Yellow Head! Yellow Head!" Billy Brogan said. "I'm afeerd, I'm afeerd, you're truckin' with the Wee People. You're not canny, so ye aren't. And I'd be afther venturin' a small bet meself, that afore two twelvemonthses ye'll have the same power over the boys that ye now have over the birds; ye need only r'ise yer finger and whistle, and lads 'll come flockin' about ye from the farthest ends of the parish, and a bit beyont it." To which Nuala would laugh gaily, and her uncle Pat smile happily. "I'd be puttin' in for ye meself, in throth, only I'm afeerd poor Billy Brogan 'ud have but a poor show."

"And is it forsake Ellen, ye would, Billy?" Nuala would ask mischievously.

Then Billy would fall into a reverie, and shake his head. For, since the eventful Harvest Fair, although he had, after the lapse of a few weeks, continued to bring her silent homage, and to be repaid by even greater kindness, consideration, and geniality on Ellen's part, he evidently did so because he could not help bringing her her just due, and seemed to have awakened to the fact that Ellen Burns stood upon a higher plane than ever poor Billy Brogan could hope to aspire to, and was meant for a fortunate one much greater than he.

I knew this, because, on a moonlight night three nights after the fair, to escape the solemn strictures of the neighbours in council who, in Toal's, sat upon his conduct, and to escape the still severer silence of his outraged master, Billy had quitted the company and sought me at my uncle Donal's fireside, and taken me out to walk with him on the white road, and confided to me (what I well knew) the cause of his having taken the drink too much which went to his head; and we had exchanged opinions about Ellen Burns and the Master, and mutually sympathized and condoled.

But I am wandering afield. I talked of Nuala. She was my frequent companion, I said, when I went nesting—as was she also when I went nutting or sloeing, or ginnling for trout; which latter she learnt to do almost as deftly as myself; and she very often provided her uncle Pat with a delicacy (taken from the burn) for his breakfast or dinner, or supper. It was only when we played *caman*—on Micky Thaig's mullin in summer, or on the frozen loch in winter—or when I joined in one of the Vagabone's madcap escapades, and forays, orchard-robbing and the like, that Nuala took no part; and was oftentimes even kept completely ignorant of great happenings. Also I should have mentioned that, as she bitterly resented my snaring hares and pheasants, which, she said, was very cruel, I always walked the rounds of my snares alone, and, concealed from her all evidences of my continuance of the practice—wherein, I know, I acted the part of a hypocrite; but the love of snaring had grown upon me through my child years, and I could not now deny myself the indulgence without a greater effort than suited my indolent nature. Even when, by purposely rising earlier in the morning, or otherwise meanly outwitting me, Owen-a-Slaivin contrived to reap the benefit of my skill, far from being discouraged I, at those times, felt all the incitement of a losing gamester to renewed effort.

I said I had resolved never again to run the risk of injuring one of God's birds. And this resolve, of course, laid me under no obligation whatsoever to refrain from persecution of the outcast wren. Not, indeed, that I had ever borne it a tithe of that bitter spite which the other youngsters loved to wreak upon it; only, as it seemed to me perfectly lawful—not actually commendable, as they thought—to harass it upon occasion, I did not take any particular pains to refrain from doing so. Neither, at the same time, did I molest it when Nuala rambled with me.

On the day after Christmas the Vagabone uttered a general ukase against the accursed bird, and summoned his liegemen all to join him in another of the many wars of extermination which he waged against the vile thummikin. Out of an old copy of a Penny Journal which he had brought with him recently from his Augherbeg exile, he had heard me read how that St. Stephen's Day was always set apart for hunting the wren by the youth of southern Ireland, and determining that it was a laudable custom, he decided that it should be introduced at Knockagar. On this particular day, then, there was a grand rally of the Vagabone's faithful followers—myself, of course, included—and the wren tribe got good reason then to conclude that the day of their extinction had at length come.

Armed with stout sticks, and pocketsful of stones, we chased it from bush to bush, and from wall to wall, even tearing down walls to drive it from its refuge, pursuing it with a malignant spite which was deepened by the aggravating way it had of disappearing through a crevice only one-fourth its own size, in a stone wall. And if any further proof of its being under the protection of the devil, as his very own bird, were needed, this was afforded fifty times and five that day, when (as the Vagabone was prepared to affirm on oath, "on any Bible in the land"), after being struck a *polthog* fit to kill a bull, it flew off unconcernedly to the next bush, leaving us gazing after it, and gazing at each other, in open-mouthed amazement.

We made the hills and the scrugs noisy that day, for when a fresh one was raised, or an escaped one rediscovered, we shouted like fox-hunters—only rather more strenuously, and we bounded and tumbled over each other in the mad rush for vengeance upon the evil bird, and upon its Master; for every wren killed meant a rib broken in the Devil.

We were fairly successful, returning in the

evening with five birds tied to the triumphal pole which the Vagabone bore in front of us, and carried around Knockagar to exhibit to all, amid our cheers of victory.

But as the procession marched up Pat's lane, it was met and stopped midway by Nuala, who had come running down to find what was the matter. There grew over her face an expression of pain when she laid her eyes on the bodies of the little birds dangling from the pole. And when I saw that I slunk to the rear.

She spoke scathingly to young Toal, and ordered him to proceed no farther.

"Woman, dear," said Toal tolerantly, "ye don't ondherstand. We've bruck five ribs in the Divil the day, and it's your Uncle Pat 'll be the glad man to know it. We're only goin' up to let him see them. Get out of our road."

"Go away out of this, Toal-a-Gallagher," she said angrily, "my Uncle Pat 'll take a stick to yous. Go away! for it's beasts ye are instead of boys, to go murdering the poor innocents wrans like that."

"The—poor—innocent—wrans!" said Toal, looking round at his followers with an expression of amused scorn. And all his followers laughed a loud and scornful laugh at the sublimity of poor Nuala's innocence.

"Innocent wrans!" Toal said, addressing Nuala,

"do you think am I innocent?" he asked scornfully. "Owen-a-Slaivin says," he went on with the proud confidence of one who has easily the best of an argument, "that there's seven divils in me, every wan of them the size of a hedgehog. And as sure as there is then there's seventeen divils in the body of a wran, the smallest of them as big as Matthew McCourt's bull. The—poor—innocent—wrans! Nuala Gildea, have a little gumption, and stan' out of our roads."

But Nuala, eschewing further verbal argument with the Vagabone, knit her brows, and, putting her two hands against him, shoved him back against the ranks of his men, who laughed at their leader for being thus staggered by a woman.

"I tell ye, don't do that," Toal said, with an assumed ferocity that should have daunted a bigger woman, "and stan' owra * that, owra me road."

But Nuala, with grim determination, advanced on him again, and with both hands gave him another shove that threw him back upon the ranks once more, and drew cries of derisive laughter that stung the Vagabone. He cast a fierce glance upon his retainers, and hissed, "Let no man laugh again that hasn't stickin'-plaster in his pockets." Then, to Nuala, "If ye don't get owra that, and not try

* Out of.

that thrick again, I'll—I'll—I'll—I know what I'll do," furiously.

But his warning word to his retainers was so significant that no one did laugh—audibly, at least—or let the faintest sound of enjoyment escape when Nuala threw him backward again.

Mortification and anger had strong possession of the Vagabone now, and he glanced furiously at Nuala.

"Och," he said furiously, "I wisht to goodness ye were a man." It was evident he was resolved to give up the contest, since his own rude chivalry would not permit him to do anything so undignified as to wrestle with a weak woman. So, as a parting shot, he shook his clenched fist at her, saying, "Ye—ye—ye yalla-haired wee imp-o-the-divil, ye! If I was your uncle I'd taich ye manners on the bare legs with a sally rod!"

But at this point Nuala's pent-up feelings gave way. She hung her head, and hastily brushed her eyes with the back of her hand, yet made no murmur.

I had felt for Nuala all through, reading (as I could) the repressed feeling pictured in her face while she strove to drive the Vagabone away; yet, partly because she was decidedly getting the best of it, but chiefly perhaps because I was seized with the desire to conceal myself, I had not made any demonstration of sympathy, and did not intend to do so. On the instant, though, that I saw her draw her hand across her eyes, I sprang forward wrathfully and struck the Vagabone a fierce box on the side of the head, which sent him staggering against the ditch. When he recovered himself he looked at me for just a moment, puzzledly; then saying, "Thanks be to Goodness!" bounded lightly into the field by the lane side, where he had divested himself of his coat and waistcoat, and had his muffler knotted around his loins in less time than I can take to tell it. One minute later I was standing up to him in like fashion, and with the exception of three boys who remained on the ditch to keep Nuala at bay, the remainder of our fellows formed a ring around us.

Seeing that we paused, young Matt McCourt, knowing well what we waited for, sang out:

"Who dar say 'bread'?"

"'Bread'!" we both chorused.

"Now, then, pull three hairs out of his head," said Matt, pursuing the usual poetic formula.

And thereupon both of us created a *casus belli* by attempting thrice thirty-three, rather than the minimum three. And the next minute we were, to the intense delight of the encouraging ring, hitting out straight from the shoulder, and swinging and slashing in fine style.

There is no doubt that the Vagabone was far my superior as a boxer; for he was hardier, and he, moreover, boxed almost every day (from pure love of boxing), whilst I boxed but very seldom—and then, generally, because I could not help it. But the fierceness with which I had been inspired by the sight of the yellow-haired Nuala in tears compensated in large measure for lack of experience; and, whilst in the savage joy of fighting I felt from the Vagabone's blows only a pleasurable sensation, I drove home my own with a force that made him yield his ground again and again, and drew shouts of delighted approval from the crowd.

I do not know how it would have ended, but fancy that Toal's superior hardiness and staying powers would have carried the day, if the fight had not been so suddenly interrupted, a big grasp being unexpectedly laid on the collars of both, tearing us asunder. When we looked up, we found the Widow's Pat shaking a reproachful head at us. For Nuala, being defeated in her object of getting into the field to separate us herself, had run to the house and alarmed Pat of what was in progress.

Even now she was at her uncle's elbow, her face betraying much trouble and alarm.

"A purty pair of boys yous are!" said Pat, sorrowfully. "Yous ought to feel heartily ashamed of yourselves! To be squabblin' and fightin' like a pair of crosst cats!"

"I don't think Dinny's so much to blame—altogether," Nuala said.

The "altogether" stung me a little, and I cast a reproachful look upon her.

"Well, Dinny," she replied to my look, tossing her head with a suggestion of defiance, "ye know ye helped to kill the poor wrans just as well as Toal or any of them."

I said: "I suppose, Nuala, ye think ye'll make me say I am sorry I took your part. But I'm not," scathingly, "and I'd fight Toal over again for it." Toal, hereupon, struggled in Pat's grasp, but vainly.

"No, Dinny O'Friel, I don't want to make ye say any suchan a thing. But I'm sorry ye fought for me, all the same, and you'd make me very angry it ye'd do it again," Nuala replied.

"Then, Nuala, if ye only take away yer uncle, I'll very soon make ye mad angry," I said warmly.

"For shame, Dinny! For shame, Dinny! And for shame you, too, Toal-a-Gallagher!" Pat said. For the Vagabone was writhing in endeavours to get free.

"Yes, uncle, it's shame for the two of them," Nuala said.

"Shake hands, and be done with it," said Pat.

I promptly extended a hand to the Vagabone, looking him boldly in the eye; and he, without any hesitation, took my hand, and returned the look. We were instantly as thorough friends as we had ever been.

"That's right," said Pat, triumphantly, as he freed both of us. "Now come up and wash the blood off yourselves. Yous is the heart and sowl of two manly fellas—that's what yous is!"

The others cheered us, and as we stepped up the hill after Pat we both felt very proud. Nuala stepped out beside me, and enclasped my arm in both of hers as we went.

"I know you're angry with me, Dinny," she said, looking up into my face, "and it isn't my fault. I had to say the truth of my mind. Of course, I thank ye very, very much for meanin' well by me, but—"

"Nuala," I said, as gently as I could, "I didn't do it for thanks, and I don't want any; and I wish you wouldn't talk about thanks. I done it because I couldn't help it. There now."

"Dinny," she said, after a minute's silence, "ye are very, very good—only, why did ye help them to kill the poor wrans?" pleadingly.

"Nuala," I said, "its the divil's bird—the wran's the divil's bird."

"I don't believe it," she said promptly and

warmly. "Every one of the birds is God's birds —that's what they are. Every one of them."

"Well, ask your uncle Pat," said I.

After the Vagabone and I had washed, and were looking like civilised beings and Christians once more, we got the choice seats by the bright fire. All the other lads sat, some around the fire with us, and some around the walls. And Pat enlightened Nuala and such others as were in ignorance why the wren was the Devil's bird.

Pat said: "It was the time the sojers were lookin' for our Saviour to kill him. He walked over a field where a man was sowin' whait, and there was drops of blood fell from our Saviour as he walked across it, and by a miracle the whait sprang up all in wan night and was ripe and ready for shearin' nixt day. And on this nixt day the sojers came by, the same way, on the s'arch for Him. There was a robin on a thorn bush in the whait fiel' seen the sojers comin'. It lay upon every dhrop of blood that marked our Saviour's thrack and didn't leave a thrace of it for the sojers to folly—which is the raison that from that day to this the robin has a rud breast. The captain of the sojers axed the robin if it had seen a man passin' that way lately. 'Not,' says the robin, 'since that whait was sown.' 'At that rate,' says the captain of the sojers, 'we're on the wrong thrack.' And he had his men turned and was marchin' off with them, when the wran comes flyin' up and says, 'The whait was sown yestherday! The whait was sown yestherday!' And with that the sojers was wheeled again, and away over the whait fiel', and niver stopped till they come up with our Saviour. And from that day the wran was cursed; and iver since it has been hunted and parsecuted."

"And it couldn't get half enough parsecution," the Vagabone said warmly. "Of all the birds in the sky," he added, "I niver did turn a feather on the robin rudbreast."

"No wan iver did, or iver would," said Pat.

"And I'm very sure," the Vagabone continued, "that I'll niver do so now I know the rale raison why it's a holy bird—and yet, Divil's bird and miserable wee object as the wran is, it's the king of all birds."

"Ay, and it carries another curse for that," I said.

"It does. It carries Colm Cille's curse for that," Pat said. "Up till St. Colm Cille's days there was no right agreement among the birds as to which of them should be king; and this caused no end of trouble, and of squabblin' and fightin' among them. So, at long and at last, they agreed to come together and choose a king. But when they did come together from all ends of the earth they found themselves as far from agreein' as ever; till wan of them proposed that they should all go to Colm Cille—for the goodness of the Sent, and the way the birds and the animals of Donegal and Derry loved him was known to the corners of land and say.

"Sent Colm Cille he agreed to be judge atween them, and he called around him from the four winds of the wurrl' every known and unknown bird, and he addhressed them, and sayed that he would wanst and for all decide upon their king, and that bird who'd fly highest would get the honour.

"All of them acknowledged this would be both fair and just, and that they'd ever after abide by it. Then he started them to fly, and they weren't far up till first wan bird dropped out, and then another, and another, and so on, till at long last the aigle only seemed to be left; and when he reached his very highest, not able to move another feather, up there starts from his back (where the desaivin' rascal had been sittin' unnoticed all the time) a wran, and mounted a few feet higher in the sky, and then come down, the king of all birds!

"The Sent of course had to abide be his own rulin', but if he had, itself, he then and there cursed it for its thrickery, that it might never again fly higher above the earth than what it flew above the aigle's back; and that is why, to this day, it always flies jookin', jookin', the height of a man's knee above the ground."

"'Twas the desarvin' of it, the divil's imp!" the Vagabone said. And around the walls they said, "Ay, it's rich desarvin'."

But Nuala asked Pat, "How long ago since all them things happened, Uncle Pat?"

"Atween a thousand and two thousand years," Pat replied.

"And if it's under Colm Cille's curse, and persecuted for more than a thousand years," Nuala said, "don't ye think the poor wee wran has paid for all its mischief?"

"I think that," Pat said. "We disputed it in John Burns's not wan month ago. John, he sayed its sin would be visited on its offspring's offspring to all ginirations. I disputed it, but Toal and Owen-a-Slaivin backed John's opinion."

"What did Ellen say?" I asked eagerly.

"Oh!" Pat said, "Ellen she agreed with me that it had doubly and thrubly ped for its sin, and shouldn't be parsecuted no more."

"I thought so," I said triumphantly. "And for my part, I'll niver trouble it any more."

Nuala came behind me where I sat upon a creepy-stool, wound her arms around my neck, and said, "Thanky, thanky, ever so much, Dinny."

"I don't care, Nuala Gildea," the Vagabone, in

reply to this demonstration, said with earnest sincerity; "afther all we've heerd, I'll niver have any aisy night's sleep while I know there's a wran wantin' fear put intil its little black sowl, in the lan'.'

CHAPTER XVI.

BY THE YALLA FIRELIGHT.

WHEN I had done my evening's work, in the field, alongside Uncle Donal, or (on wet days) about the house and the byre, and then spent an hour or more at my books—stretched out by the fireside—I very frequently, as I told before, went out on my *céilidh* to one or other of the neighbours' houses. Frequently, but not always. Though Uncle Donal, for my sake, loved to see me happy, and therefore gave me not only full liberty but even encouragement to take a few hours' relaxation among the neighbours; yet for his own sake he loved—though he thought he hid this from me—to have me sit with him by our own fireside, of a night; sometimes to sit in happy silence whilst he smoked and watched the fire, and sometimes, when he was in that mood, to sit in chat. At these times great old chats we would have; for he spoke to me gravely and sagely as to a young man. And on most topics he spoke fully and freely to me, which he never did to the neighbours, in whose presence he was taciturn. All this flattered me much, for I felt more mature than perhaps my years warranted, and certainly more than those would credit me who assembled in Toal's or John's. Consequently after a good, pleasing chat, in which my uncle treated me as one worthy of a man's confidence, and as one capable of forming opinions upon grave subjects, I always retired to bed feeling more a man and less a child than I had done a very few hours before. And I knew that my uncle saw into my breast as other grown people did not, and saw that I was not merely a thoughtless boy, but one who observed and weighed and reflected.

Of course, all my own comrades, particularly Nuala, tacitly acknowledged this. The Vagabone thought that from much serious reading a fine trickster was in imminent danger of being lost in me.

On a night when I closed my books finally and half arose from my flat postuie by the fire, Uncle Donal, who had been sitting opposite to me for the last hour, smoking and watching me intently, took the pipe from his mouth and remarked as he saw me rub my eyes:

"Dinny, *a thaisge*,* I'm afeered ye bother your eyes too much with the books."

"No, Uncle Donal," I said, "you needn't be afeerd of that."

"Why don't you use the rush oftener, and the fire less."

"Och, I would sooner have the light of the fire. You have trouble makin' the rush-lights, and they serve yourself best. For me, if I was readin' by them, or gettin' a lesson by them, they somehow or another take away a whole lot of the beauty of the book, or interest of the lesson, that I can find so plenty when the yalla firelight does be dancin' over the pages. And the firelight alone always makes me feel far happier and contenteder."

My Uncle Donal looked at me for a minute, and then said, "Ye're a sthrange boy, surely, Dinny. And it's your poor mother (God be marciful to her!) that I often see lookin' from the eyes, and spaikin' from the mouth, of ye."

"What's sthrange, Uncle Donal?" I asked remonstratingly. "Is it my thinkin' that bonny leapin' blaze there finer and lovelier than a smoky rush-light? Or would it be so very sthrange if I sayed it was finer and lovelier far than any other light?"

---

* Treasure.

"No, I suppose it shouldn't be sthrange, Dinny," he said.

"Do ye know, uncle, often and often when I'm lying stretched there, readin' some lovely passage by the yalla firelight, I fall a-wondherin' about how they do in big cities and away out of Irelan', where there's no turf and fir for burnin'—and wondherin' about how much of the happiness of a pleasant book the young fellas in them places must lose."

"God bliss ye, Dinny," my uncle replied. But there was a watery glint in his eyes.

Both of us remained silent, looking into the blaze on the hearth, for a short time. At length I said:

"With you, Uncle Donal, and with that fire and my books I think I could be always happy."

My uncle did not make any reply, and when I looked up I saw, by the gleam of the firelight on them, that his eyes were filled and welling over. I dropped my gaze to the hearth again immediately, and puzzled over the meaning of it.

After a while Uncle Donal said, with deep feeling in his tone, "May God always keep your heart young, Dinny, and bright and happy."

I bowed my head in acquiescence of the good prayer.

"Me ye can't have for long, now, Dinny. To have that fire and your books ye'll have to sthruggle, poor fella."

"Don't say that, Uncle Donal," I expostulated. "Of course, I'll have ye for long and long." I had never before seriously contemplated losing him, and I could not now bear to have the reflection forced upon me.

"Oh, Dinny," he said, "but ye must know it; ye must take it to heart, for your own sake. In years I'm gettin' purty ould now; and I'm oulder still than me years," and he shook his head sorrowfully as he said this. "Then, Dinny, when I go ye'll surely have to sthruggle with the wurrl'—maybe afore I go. Maybe! maybe!—Dinny, you don't know, I don't know, how soon ye'll have to begin that sthruggle."

I was listening intently.

"That's why I always like to see ye at your books. I don't like the thoughts of ye, me poor Dinny, goin' out to fight the wurrl' with nothin' but your two bare hands. It's a rough wurrl', Dinny—it's a rough wurrl'. I know it. You'll find it out. I had to fight it with me hands—through me own fault, me own fault! And if a man has to—has to—fight a losin' battle, and knowin' it's a losin' battle, he—he —well, Dinny, I pray to God from me heart that such may niver be your misfortune!"

"Amen! Uncle."

"Anyhow, Dinny," he went on, heaving a sigh of relief, "as I sayed, I can't bear to think of you beginnin' to wrastle with the wurrl' as I've wrastled with it—liven' with your back doubled, and your two ends in the earth from Cuckoo to Cuckoo. And that's why I love to see ye at your books of a night—in hopes that you'll make somethin' of them yet."

"I hope I will, Uncle," I said.

"My father was poor," Uncle Donal spoke reflectively, "but he had the respect for the larnin'. Bekase I was bright and quick at uptakin', when I come to the time of day to be a use and a help till him, he willingly denied himself of me. There was a day in late Spring—a dirty, miserable, cowl' day it was, too—for well I mind it—that we turned the last spadeful on the seed, and I sayed, as I straightened me back and rubbed the cowl' sleet off me face with me sleeve, I sayed, 'Thank God that the last of them's set, and I'm not sorry. 'Donal,' says me father, says he, 'if ye like to choose another life, ye can start South the morra', in God's name.' And as suddint as me father put it to me, so suddint did I decide. 'In God's name I will, father,' says I. And on the very next mornin', with fewer rags of clothes nor I'll say, and a couple of simple books, tied up in a handkerchief, and with me father and mother's blissin' (all they could give me), I set me face south, where the Larnin' was, and I thravelled afore me. I couldn't clink four pennies in me pocket—but neither did I need them, for there was none so mean as to take payment for his bed, or his bite and his sup, from the Poor Scholar.

"I thravelled for a fortnight till I come intil the County Clare, to a taicher whose fame was known for four weeks' distance from him, Murtach MacNamara. And though his school was, in the winter time in the corner of a barn given by some wan for God's sake and the sake of Larnin', and in the summer time undher a hedge, Murtach MacNamara turned out scholars that took their place among the brightest stars of Irelan', and scholars that were afterwards famous in the univarsities of France and Spain.

"Undher him I started what I prayed God (and what me poor father and mother at home were prayin' God) might be a successful career. And Murtach, afore I was a week with him toul' me it was in my power if I only worked with a will, to add another p'arl to his crown—so he put it. And this give me heart to work harder and harder; which I did. And the way I stuck to me books give them a likin' to me everywhere I stopped—for, like all Poor Scholars, I went week about to the houses of the other scholars. But there was wan house I went oftener to, and found a warmer welcome in than any of the others, and that was the house of Cathal Hayes: and Cathal's daughter Mary, who was far on in her books though she was younger than meself, she was a great help to me entirely, and used to put me through me lessons, be the fire, every night. And black-haired Mary Hayes was a merry-hearted girl, who loved to banther me often; and she'd say, 'Some day, Donal, when your're a bishop, it's me 'ill be the proud woman that can boast it was me helped to make the bishop out of ye.' She'd laugh at this joke, and I'd laugh at it, too. And we'd have many a great chat by the fire, when our lessons was over, for Mary had a big intherest in me, and she'd have me tellin' her histhory-passages out of me life that she was so fond of hearin' she'd sit till cock-crow in the mornin' listenin' to them if I'd consent. I used to thank God that give me such a kind sister; and I used to say to meself that when, with God's help, I'd be a priest, I would pay Mary back for all her goodness to me.

"Dinny, you're young and don't rightly understand these things yet: but, anyhow, without either of us intendin' it, or ever dhreamin' such a thing could happen, we suddenly found ourselves fonder of other than we should be; and when we did find this, it was a heart-br'ak to both of us, for while we couldn't keep asunder we knew every time we come together was makin' it harder for us to think of ever partin'.

"But Cathal Hayes very soon—for he couldn't be blind—seen how matters had got. He hinted to me as gently as he could that it was better for me not to put up at his house more. This did'nt remedy things, though, for where there's a will there's a way. So, the next thing, Cathal gave me warnin' to lave the county, for he couldn't be disgraced be a Poor Scholar marryin' a daughter of his. I wanted to go, God knows, afore ever he gave me the warnin', and I prayed to God to give me the sthren'th to go—but God didn't see fit to lift me out of the way of me punishment. So it was that I still remained on, till Cathal met me on the road alone wan day, and fell on me with his whip. When he give me a cut of it across the face, callin' me a damned beggar, the blood boiled in me veins, and I lost all conthrol of meself, and all knowledge of what I was doin'—I only saw him lyin' unconscious on the road when I turned and left him. May God forgive me!" my uncle Donal ejaculated this with a painful intensity, and he remained silent for a few minutes after.

Then he went on: "I went away, and stayed in the next barony for three weeks, till I heard that Cathal Hayes was recovered and was well again. I ventured back quietly, and I sent to Mary a very humble message beggin' she'd meet me till I would tell her the sorrow that was bitin' me heart, for havin' even in me madness laid a finger on wan that was a drop's blood to her, let alone on her very father.

"But Mary would not see me, and wouldn't even send wan word of message back to me. I kept in hidin' thereabout, for three weeks longer, and sent many messages to Mary, for she wasn't to be seen out herself. To the messengers she wouldn't part her lips, only waved them away with her hand—like that. And they toul' me she looked both frightfully pale and worn. After three weeks there came to me wan mornin' the Hayes' sarvant girl. It made me heart leap with hope when I seen her comin'—with a hope that wasn't long lastin', Dinny, for she come to tell me that Mary had sailed for France, for a convent school there, at midnight the night afore, in a smugglin' smack; that she went of her own free will, and that she bid the little girl come to me and say two words, and no more, 'Farewell, Donal!'"

My uncle remained silent now for several minutes, his head between his hands, his elbows resting on his knees, and he gazing into the fire.

"Dinny," he resumed again, "I wouldn't wish it to me worst enemy to suffer what I suffered afther hearin' that. I couldn't be brought to look at a book afther. I pitched me books to the winds, and I took to frequentin' still-houses, strivin' (may God forgive me!) to dhrownd my great throuble in dhrink. Plenty of them that used to take an intherest in me sthruv to make me start for home. But that I couldn't do; for I had closed me mind to father and mother and all at home, and wouldn't let meself even think of them for two minutes together.

"I sunk, Dinny—sunk—sunk. But God didn't let me parish. I didn't know then, what I knew afterwards, that me poor mother never let pass wan night that she didn't lead the house in a rosary for me. And God's heart heerd that rosary.

"Afore I left home the Unitin' had been goin' on for a good while, and I, as every young Irishman should, had joined the Unitin' Men*, in the expectations of sthrikin' for Irelan', on the great and long-looked-for day when all would be ripe and ready. And when I came to Clare I didn't altogether forget it, notwithstandin' me books and me new aims.

"But lately I wanted to forget that, as I wanted to forget everything else that would make for good

*The United Irishman organization, which spread to all corners of the Island in the Nineties, and terminated in the Insurrection of 1798.

in me life—wanted to forget it, and nearly succeeded, as I thought.

"But wan May night, afther I'd been three months leadin' a sorry life, I was sittin' in a still-house half dazed, as I was all that time, when we heard a horse come gallopin' at top speed and stop short at the doore, and a man burst in, and he hatless and breathless, and shouted, 'Men, this is no time for idlin' in still-houses. Lord Edwards in jail and dyin' of pistol shots and bayonet stabs! But the Boys are Up in Kildare, and are fightin' for Freedom or Daith!'

"Dinny, I was me oul' self again, the ins'ant I heerd the words. Four other lads joined me, and off for Kildare we started. But when we reached there we were just in time to get the first word of the surrender on the Hill of Allen, and the massacre of three hundred and fifty defenceless people at the Gibbet-Rath, on the currach. We had come fired with hope, but now we were frozen with despair. We lay in hidin' for several days, till we got the word that Wexford was Up. And by stolen night-marches we reached Wexford and joined the Boys at Carrickburne Hill just as they mustered to march on New Ross. And next day, when our messenger was shot by Mountjoy's men, I was one of the crowd of pikemen that, without waitin' for a word of command, threw ourselves again the town, swept the English cavalry back upon the infantry, and drove both of them pell-mell out over the bridge, leavin' the town and the artillery in our hands."

"Uncle Donal," I cried with enthusiasm, "how gloryus that must 'a' been!"

"Dinny," said my uncle, "I'd give all the rest of me life for wan other such gloryus hour."

"I don't doubt it, uncle—I don't doubt it," I said reflectively. "I wish, and wish, that in poor Ireland's cause the chance may be mine to make such a dash some day, and see the red-coats flyin'!"

Uncle Donal laid a hand very gently on my head and kept it there a wee while. I knew he was looking down on me with loving pride in his eye—I knew this, though I did not see it; for I was gazing far into the fire.

"God grant your wish, Dinny, *a stor*," he said, "and may He speed it."

I said, "Amen, Uncle."

My uncle went on, "What happened in New Ross afther, ye know yourself, Dinny?"

"I know it. I've read it often," I said, with a sorrowful head-shake.

"Thank God," he said from his heart, "bad as I had been, I tasted no dhrink that day. But I wrought my level best doin' what I could to pay my share of the score we owed the British for all the scoundrelism I had seen them practise on the Unitin' men and their families in the North. If every man had done his part as well, we'd 'a' been square with them.

"Well, I was into many a scrimmage afther, atween then and the day of Vinegar Hill, and we generally done good work. But there was the wan grand mistake workin' again' us, all the time—the want of organization and discipline, and obedience. So that, always what we won with wan hand we lost with the other.

"And afther the big day of Vinegar Hill, when Wexford women showed as dauntless courage as ever the men did, it was plain that the game was up —which it never would been if the Wexford men had been officered. So, with no worse nor a broken arm, I went into hidin', with two of the Clare boys —the other two were killed, wan at New Ross, and the other in the Wexford hospital, where every wounded man was put to death when the English troops poured intil the town.

"Afther bein' on our keepin', wan place and another, here, for a week, till we seen there wasn't the last flicker of hope, we stole out of the county. We joined a hopeless scrimmage or two in Kilkenny, and, though some wanted to persuade us to go to Wicklow with them, we knew the folly of it, and took our way for home, thravelin' be night, as afore —which ended my part in the Risin' of '98.

"When I reached back, any more than while I was gone, I wouldn't let liquor part me lips, I thank God. I then thried hard, and very hard, to put meself to me books again. But the thought of Mary Hayes, that was stronger than ever on me, now I come back, made it next to impossible to keep me mind fixed on any other thing for three minutes together. But I brought back with me a great dale of detarmination—so much that it narved me to sthruggle and sthrive for three months, with very very little success. And at the end of that time the word come, be a smugglin' smack, that Mary Hayes was dead!

"From the hour she sailed, the news was, she had done no good. She pined and failed day afther day. When she reached France the Nuns sayed she'd very soon revive, but she only grew worse and worse. Then, they sayed she should return home, and it might do her good. But she shook her head at this and wouldn't hear of it, nor would'nt tell them why. And still she failed away, till, five months after she'd seen the last of the county Clare, she closed her eyes for ever. And just afore she died they axed her had she any messages. She sayed, 'I have two. Give to me poor father the love of a lovin' daughter, and give to Donal O'Friel the love of his broken-hearted Mary.'

"In three days afther," my uncle went on, after a little, "leavin' books and masther, I turned me back on the County Clare for ever, and travelled home to Donegal. I left it, a bright and lively youth as any in the countryside, and I come back—what I have since remained, a silent man. Father and mother and neighbours and friends naturally wondered what great thing had come over me. But they never heerd. That I had been through the Wexford Troubles they soon l'arnt; but nothin' more—though they knew there was somethin' far more behind. You, Dinny, are the first that ever heerd my story.

"Dinny, Dinny, I want you to watch yourself and be always good and always careful—and always, always mind your books, and try to make better out of them than what I've done. And try to be able to do somethin' for yourself afore long—for," he said with a sigh and reflectively, "God only knows how soon ye may need it. God bliss ye, Dinny!"

My uncle went out to fodder the cows before preparing for bed; and I remained looking into the fire. The rumour of his having been in the Rising I had frequently heard among the neighbours. His intense love for Ireland I had always known—always felt; for, though on this as on any other subject he said little, he somehow made all around him feel his sentiments in all their fervour. Yet I had not hitherto had my belief that he was an actor in the Rebellion authoritatively confirmed. Now Uncle Donal was in my eyes truly a hero, about whom I could weave fine fancies and dream proud dreams. The great misfortune, too, which changed all his life, though I could not then realize the full depth of its sadness, invested him with a pitying interest for me. So he was of the most prized heroes—a hero that claimed sympathy.

When my uncle returned from the byre, I was mechanically tracing lines in the ashes of the hearth with the tongs; and I started as from sleep when he patted me on the head and said: "The Rosary, Dinny, the Rosary. Ye must be up early and out with the cows for an hour afore br'akfast."

CHAPTER XVII.

WHEN CORNEY DREW HIS PENSION.

WITHOUT admitting that I had harboured revenge against Toal a-Gallagher for the strapping he gave me on the night we discussed Colm Cille's prophecies, I will say that I was not averse to wiping out the score when opportunity offered.

The opportunity did offer on a day when Corney Higarty drew his pension: and I then balanced accounts. Though—as was often the case with me—when it was done, I was sorry.

It was always a great day for Knockagar when Corney drew his pension. In particular it was a great day for his cronies. Usually, the stream of life moved on unruffled, unvaried, and always pleasantly, with us; but, four times in the year there was for Corney's friends a sudden and not unpleasant agitation in the stream. These were Corney's pension days, when money was as plentiful as March wind, and ran as freely as the Roe water, when every thirsty soul who claimed friendship there, had his claims magnanimously allowed in Corney's cabin, where, around a dancing fire-flame, the social glass sped, bosoms were unlocked, and tongues were loosed.

On the particular occasion—it was an April evening—of which I now speak, Corney had been to Donegal to draw his two pound eight and nine-pence; he had had Pat with him, and Pat's donkey and cart, in which he brought back the many parcels that were on every returning quarter-day the wonder and mystery and fruitful source of speculation to the womankind of Knockagar in general, and to Susie Gallagher in particular. That one of the parcels contained a jar of whisky was of course as certain as that another contained butcher's meat—that rarity at Knockagar, the consumption of which raised Corney temporarily to the social attitude of Father Dan, the only other person in our community who could (occasionally) afford the extravagant luxury. Thus the contents of two only of the parcels were removed from the field of speculation. There was no saying what presents for his favourites amongst the youngsters constituted another parcel, what new shirts and socks a fourth, what shop-cloth for a new coat, or delft-ware for his dresser; perhaps he had speculated upon a new skillet, or invested in a pair of tongs, or bought a patchwork quilt to adorn his bed; and, over and above all they could think of, it was pretty positive that Pat's car bore home to him some domestic convenience, that by its unexpectedness and novelty was destined to startle Knockagar—for Corney, like all men who have more money than they know what to do with, fancied new and rare things, and felt a harmless gratification in the exclusive possession of them. The self-possession, almost rising to indifference, with which the Widow's Pat, striding along beside the cart, bore in his bosom the full knowledge of this load of mysteries, was a matter of astonishment, and in one less esteemed than he would assuredly have been a matter of aggravation, to all our womankind.

I and many other youths who expecting presents in award for favours done, had been lying in wait for the convoy two good miles beyond Knockagar, proudly accompanied it on its progress through the village. Ellen Burns, who was at the window, basting for her father, looked out and smiled benignly on Corney and the convoy, and Corney who was ever a soldier and gallant on such a day, replied with his gravest and most admirable military salute. Matthew McCourt's Bess, who had evidently been waiting for us, came, can in hand, meeting us, on pretence of going to John Burns' Well, but only too obviously with real intent of getting a good look into the cart in passing. Susie Gallagher, indeed, in whom the inquisitive instinct was very highly developed, walked out of her house direct, looked into the cart, and turning to Corney, hazarded, after her own fashion, "I know that's a fryin'-pan ye have in the flat parcel? But it's more a puzzle to me what ye have in the two square wans atop of it?" Then she fixed him with her seldom-failing eye, whilst she paused for his reply.

"Ma'am," Corney replied calmly, "it needn't be more a puzzle to ye any longer; for, ye know just about as much what's in the square wans as what's in the flat wan. And ye know about as little what's in the flat wan, as what's in the square wans." For Corney (because he had been abroad) entertained the idea that curiosity should be kept within reasonable bounds; and because of this, Susie's inquisitiveness had often been a cause of ire to him —of carefully repressed ire. Indeed, to tell truth, but that he was a bit pot-valiant just now, he would not have dared this reply.

"Corney Higarty," Susie, when she had recovered herself, replied to him with infinite disdain, "if ye only had a little more manners and a great deal less imper'ence, ye might be fit for the society of Christians."

Corney did not even deign to halt for the purpose

of bandying words with this woman. But he said over his shoulder, "Since ye're so familiar with the mains, it's a wondher to me ye niver practised them, ma'am."

Susie's feelings thereat were too deep for words, for after she had followed him with a long look she turned in silence, and went into the house.

"Pat," said Corney, elatedly, "how did I do that?"

"I think, Corney," Pat pleaded, "ye were rather too sharp with poor Susie." For Pat was ever the champion of the defeated.

Corney was disappointed, for he had expected Pat's encomiums.

"Patrick," he said, gravely, "thick hides needs sharp waipons."

To this Pat wisely made no reply. And Corney carried his head inordinately high in the air till he reached home.

Amongst the presents he had brought with him were The History of Freney the Robber and a penny for me, a brooch and a schoolbag—the first seen in Knockagar—that opened and closed on a running string, for Nuala; a pretty flowered muslin tie for Ellen Burns, and a ballad for Billy Brogan. My pleasure at being made the bearer of the latter three presents was only exceeded by my delight in the possession of my own.

Later in the evening Corney's friends would

gather to help him celebrate the occasion, but just now he must appease the ravenous appetite which was the combined result of a long fast, several nips of whiskey and the possession of fresh beef. So, while he prepared the potatoes in a skillet, he boiled the beef in a kettle. The Widow's Pat had, against Corney's will, gone home, to partake of his own humble meal at his own fireside; and, since Corney enjoyed a good meal doubly when he had good company to share it, Owen a-Slaivin was (not unwillingly) pressed into service for the occasion. The potatoes came off the fire laughing through their jackets; the soup, as spooned from the kettle by Corney and Owen alternately, was unanimously declared perfect, and the shank of beef, when experimentally prodded, was declared done to a turn. So the kettle, too, was linked off, but, to Owen's consternation and Corney's great aggravation, the meat, having swollen in cooking, obstinately refused to be enticed or forced from the narrow kettle-mouth, though both Owen and Corney endeavoured to coax and to coerce it in turn. As the effort was very trying on their patience, they had frequent recourse to the whiskey bottle, to sooth their feelings and give them new determination. When matters were at their worst, and Corney's temper and the kettle were both in imminent danger of breaking, a long, loud and hearty laugh that suddenly burst overhead startled the two who laboured with the stubborn beef and provoking kettle; and, looking up they saw the mischievous face of the Vagabond peering down at them through the aperture in the roof end, which answered the purpose of a chimney.

With an alacrity that was wonderful for him, Corney bounded to the door, tore it open and dashed out. But at Corney's first move the face had instantly disappeared from the roof opening. Owen heard a thud on the ground, and immediately after the angry pursuing cries of his friend Corney.

Owen had the beef extricated when, after a time, the indignant Corney stalked in again.

"Some day," Corney said grimly, "some day I'll thraw the neck of thon young divil's imp." He illustrated the threat by grasping an imaginary something with his left hand, and pulling with a twist another imaginary something with his right hand.

"Ye didn't ketch him?" said Owen.

"I didn't ketch him," Corney said regretfully. "He has as many twists in him as a gimlet. But if the Lord sends that I get me hands on him afore the hangman, the hangman'll be chaited for wanst. But I went to his mother," said Corney.

"Ye did?" said Owen.

"I did," Corney said decisively. "And I got rid of a piece of me mind to her—a good piece of it."

"Hagh!" said Owen, approvingly.

"I was glad of the chance of gettin' at her, for she had the imper'ence to try to taich me manners this very day, as me and Pat come home," Corney said.

"I thrust in the Lord ye give it till her sore, Corney," Owen said. For bitter remembrances of Susie's sharp tongue were rankling in Owen's bosom.

"I toul' her," said Corney, "she was raisin' up a young rip-rascal who was gallopin' to the gallows, with the divil afther him, at the rate of a mile a minute."

"Hagh! Good for ye, Corney! And what did Shusie say?"

"Shusie sayed—she sayed—No matther what she sayed," Corney replied. "It was only some of her own unmannerly, ill-bred, imper'ence—to which I give her her answer by sayin' it was small wondher her own son was comin' up the *teo-boy* he was, when that was the way she thraited wan who come in with a civil complaint again' him. 'Manners,' says I, 'like charity, should begin at the h'arthstone: but when the mother,' says I, 'hasn't got them, it's hard to expect them off the son.'"

"Bully for ye, Corney!" said Owen. "Bully for ye! What did Shusie say to that?"

"I don't rightly know," Corney said. "To tell

ye God's truth, Owen, I didn't stop long enough to hear. Poor Toal himself and Billy Brogan, who were workin' hard, were delighted enough to get some wan boul' enough to fetch Shusie to task. But when they heerd me givin' her that last bar, they begun twistin' their faces into more knots than they're likely to straighten out in a hurry again, mainin' for me to cut and run for it whilst there was time."

"Did ye run, Corney?" Owen asked eagerly.

"Is it *me* run?" said Corney, scornfully. "And for fear of a woman? No, Owen a-Slaivin—I didn't run!—I only walked away middlin' fast."

"Oh-h-h!" Owen said.

"Now I could ait the pads off an ass, I'm that hungry," said Corney, as he seated himself with Owen to the potatoes and beef.

When night had fallen Corney's cronies came dropping in, one by one. Big Matthew McCourt came, and John Burns, who got the seat of honour in the chimney corner, and the Widow's Pat, who got the chimney seat opposite to John, and the Master. And last of all Toal-a-Gallagher dropped in, and his man Billy, for Toal found it difficult to invent an excuse that would deceive the tyrant Susie. Indeed, it is more than likely his imagination would not have been able to cope with the difficulty had not Billy's come to his aid. For, when at length a messenger had come from Corney's and whispered his message in Billy's ear, and departed, the ever vigilant Susie demanded, "What's that young Jimmy Haraghey was whisperin' to ye, Billy?" Toal made violent faces at Billy, who, affecting not to see them, answered Susie with a cool promptitude that disarmed doubt. "He says there's a great *gar** out that Con McCadden's cow of Dhrimalusky had a calf with two heads on it this mornin'; that all the wurrl's gone to see it, and that John Burns has put on his coat and gone too, bekase he b'lieves it's wan of the signs mentioned in the Prophecy." And Toal added, "More wonderful things have been than it should be wan of the signs which is to come afore the End; for it has been foretoul' that there's to be wars and rumours of wars, and signs in the sun and moon. Billy, we'll throw on our coats and go and have a look at it."

When Toal apologised to Corney for his delay in arriving he explained how it was, thus, that they succeeded in getting away. "For, atween ourselves and the bedpost, it wouldn't be tellin' us tuppence-ha'penny of bad ha'pence if Shusie knew where we were, and what we were up to."

Then, as ever, Corney's entertaining was kingly. His stories of war, of frolic and of fight, were good, and his whiskey was, if possible, better. John

---

* Rumour.

Burns, his tongue loosed, waxed eloquent upon the fights and frays of Corney's illustrious predecessors, Brian Boru, who drove the Danes from Ireland eight hundred years before, and the redoubtable Finn McCool, who flung his spear eight hundred years earlier still. The Master in eloquent terms drew a comparison between "this far-famed warrior of modern days, whose princely hospitality it is our privilege to-night to enjoy, and the late lamented Napoleon Buonaparte—popularly known as 'Bony'" —a comparison which resulted rather to the disadvantage of the latter; and wound up by drinking Corney's health.

Toal, who was (especially when inspired by good liquor) of an independent turn of mind, condemned in no measured terms both Corney Higarty and Napoleon Buonaparte, as being two great disturbers of the world's peace—a sentiment with which Matthew McCourt outspokenly agreed. Corney Higarty took up the cudgels of defence with hearty good-will, and, outflanking the enemy, very soon turned them into those of offence. He had energetic support, too, from John Burns, who cited Joshua and Saul, and other renowned warriors of Old Testament days, to strengthen the case of Corney and Napoleon. The Master, enjoying to his heart's content the storm which he had so unexpectedly raised, leant his weight now to one side, now to the other, as he perceived either side show signs of weakening. For Toal was not beaten only because he had not the perspicuity to discover when he should be beaten; and the illogical arguments of himself, and the yet more illogical ones of his henchman, Matthew, like the concealed firing of guerillas, puzzled Corney and John far more than would better arguments if pursued logically.

Now, the Widow's Pat, who admired warriors, and was possessed of a great abstract love for peace, was pulled both ways and would go neither. But with good reason he very soon became apprehensive that Toal, who waxed hot, might easily so far forget himself as to fight for the cause of peace; so he abruptly announced, "Boys, we'll have a ballad from Billy Brogan;" and the sudden irrelevancy of this struck them, one and all, silent. "Billy," Pat went on, "give us a good, a rattlin' good, song; as it's yourself knows how." And even Billy, who had been deeply absorbed in the argument, was so taken off his guard that he had struck up his song before he recovered from his surprise. "I'll give yous the Marchant's Daughter," he said:

"In Darry lived a marchant, he had wan only daughter,
And she had sweethearts plenty to coort her night and day,
And when she had them gainéd, their company disdainéd,
And many's the clever young man, heart-wounded, went away.

"At last there came a suitor from Clady for to coort her,
With scorchin', burnin' flames to thaw her frozen heart.
Says she, 'Young man retire, your suit I don't admire,
Nor is it my desire a single life to part.

"'Your passion for me smother, and go and coort some other.'
So he went next We'nsday evenin' to wan he had in view.
He went and coorted Sally, and left disdainful Molly,
And with tears of melancholy he gave her time to rue.

"About six weeks or better she wrote to him a letter,
And he wrote her back an answer and sealed it with disdain,
Saying, 'When you could you would not, and when you would you should not,
So read these lines and grieve not, my answer is quite plain.'

"Now all ye maids take warnin' by me and my misfortune,
And never slight the young man that's master of your heart,
For if you lightly spurn him, you'll find him not returnin',
Your days you'll spend in mournin'—'tis I that feels the smart."

"Brave boy, Billy! 'Tis well ye do it!" said Pat. The Master assured him in choice terms that he was a worthy successor to the bards of old. And Toal, who proudly recognized in Billy, when praised, a bit of personal property, thanked both the Master and Pat, and the house generally, for their kind appreciation; and, having held his glass for Corney to replenish, proceeded to propose the health of everybody, making the toast a peg upon which to hang an oration. "For we're all akin to our genial host, Mr. Cornelius Higarty," Toal, in the course of his oration, said, "all sojers, in spirit if not in actiallity; and hopin' to be that in actiallity also, some day—sojers for Irelan', when Irelan' calls. And when that gloryus day comes, if it comes soon (as I from me heart pray), I'll undertake to say that the men of Knockagar will not be tadious to answer their country's call—and I'll undertake to say, further, that Toal-a-Gallagher will not be hindmost among the men of Knockagar." (Corney Higarty said "Bravo, Toal,!" and the others nodded their approval.) Toal hereupon grew more confident, and waxed more rhetorical in tone and gesture. "And on that day," he said, waving his arms, "Toal-a-Gallagher will give yous the watchword and battle-cry, 'Death or Freedom!' Away with Tyranny and"—I believe he was going to say Tyrants; but the door had suddenly opened, and Susie Gallagher, with arms akimbo, stood framed in it, and held Toal (who orated with his back to the fire and face toward the door) with an unwontedly severe eye.

"Toal-a-Gallagher," she said, in a tone the very calmness of which was pregnant with dread, "what is it ye're bletherskitin' about?" Then she paused. There was thick silence in the house.

Toal, before replying, looked around for a seat, and the Widow's Pat generously tendered the half of his straw *síostog*. When Toal found himself securely seated on this, he said, in his most appeasing manner, "Oh, just having a little talk, Shusie, dear, with Corney and the boys."

"I thought," says she, "yourself and Billy Brogan"—she here turned her eye upon Billy, who wilted under its gaze—"went for to see Con McCadden's two-headed calf of Dhrimalusky?"

Toal was painfully dumfounded.

"Do you know," said Susie, "that ye promised Father Dan his new brogues for the morra evenin'? And that this is the fif' time ye've put him off? And do ye know that Larry McGahren of Dhrimroosk is above in the house scouldin' and noratin' like a madman, about his brogues? And do ye know that ye have Tim Dorrian's leather of Fanaghan lyin' onmade, on your shelf, for eleven weeks gone, and him fit to be tied about it? And do ye know how many other people from all corners of the parish are threatenin' to come and take away their leather and give it to some wan who'll make it up for them? Do ye know that, good man—yourself and Billy Brogan?" Poor Billy fidgetted most uneasily. "And if ye do know it, is this the place for ye to be, instead of at your work-bench? In *this* house"—the emphasis on the pronoun was unmistakably meant for Corney—"in *this* house, I say, with a stove of whiskey that would knock ye down afore ye enter the doors at all. In *this* house carousin' and bletherskitin'—for it's bletherskitin' ye are best at! Come home!" said Susie. "Rise up, and come home, both of yous!" Toal arose, and Billy, and saying Good-night to Corney and the boys, walked out meekly. "Come home," said she, scathingly, as they passed her in the door,—"Come home out of this randyvoo." For she felt like laying it as heavily as possible upon Corney Higarty. She had here laid on a straw too much, though. Corney jumped to his feet, stamped on the floor, and shouted, "Ma'am, whăt did ye call my house?"

"A randyvoo, I called it," she said, turning again in the door—"A randyvoo, I called it, and a randyvoo it is."

"A—*randyvoo!*" Corney ejaculated, aghast at the enormity, and turning upon his friends appealing eyes. They inclined their heads in silent sympathy.

"A randyvoo!" Susie defiantly repeated.

"Did you hear that, Pat?" Corney appealed in martyr-tones. "Did you hear that, John Burns? and you, Matthew McCourt?"

"Put her out," Owen a-Slaivin interjected; but

in a voice so studiedly low that only his immediate neighbours heard him.

"A *randyvoo!*" Corney plaintively repeated. "Did you hear it, Masther?"

"It pains me to acknowledge that I overheard the insidious remark," the Master said boldly. For he was unquestionably daring, when necessity called.

"Upon my veracity," Corney said with decision, "I'll not let grass grow under me heels till I hear if Father Dan thinks you, Shusie Gallagher, or any other woman in the parish, or out of it, has the right to take away the character of my house."

"Tir-oodle-um!" said Susie, with affected flippancy. "Ye didn't laive it in my power to take away its character. Atween whisky-dhrinkin' every night ever you dhraw your pension, and card playin', and the Lord-only-knows-what, every other night, ye have long ago put it past the power of man or mortial to take away the character of your house. There's plain spaikin' for ye! and ye can give that in to Father Dan, too; and tell him it'll take all the Latin he knows to give your house a character again."

Corney collapsed; and the man who had faced a thousand cannon unflinchingly, before this woman subsided into his seat in utter despair.

"Shusie Gallagher!" the Widow's Pat sorrowfully said, "I'm ashamed for ye."

Owen a-Slaivin, stung into a momentary fit of reckless bravery, said, "Ye're a varaago, Shusie Gallagher!"

Susie cast a glance upon Owen that withered his spirit instantly. Then turning to the Master, she said:

"It's a wondher to me that you'd let yourself be seen in such company."

"Madam," said the Master, with judicial severity, "it is not less a wonder that you let yourself be seen in it, and heard."

"What do you mane?" Susie asked angrily.

"I mean to say, madam," said the Master, "that in my opinion you are little better than a troglodyte!"

For a moment after the bomb fell, Susie gasped for breath. Then she said, in distressful appeal, "Yous is all witnesses!"

"Little better," said the Master, with villainous coolness, applying a blazing spail of fir to his pipe —"little better," (puff) "I remarked, than a" (puff) "troglodyte."

"Master Whorisky!" she cried, "Oh, Master Whorisky! It's ill I've earned that—and from you, too. Oh! Oh! Oh!"

"It's what she is," Owen a-Slaivin said. "And

I'm prepared to swear it on any book in Europe."

Susie only said, "Oh! oh! oh!" and fled. And the Master thereat tipped the company a wink that instantly restored their good humour again.

"Friend Cornelius," said the Master, "please get the bottle into locomotion." Which order Cornelius very quickly complied with.

When Corney, two days later, called upon Father Dan to charge Susie Gallagher with an attempt at taking away the character of his house, Father Dan said gravely, "Hum! So she called it a randyvoo, did she? And what's this she's been here to tell me—but couldn't tell me—that the Masther called her?"

"He called her only her desarvin', Father Dan—a throglodyte."

The muscles about Father Dan's mouth trembled too slightly for Corney to detect the motion. After a minute Father Dan said:

"A randyvoo—a troglodyte. What are ye goin' to come to, anyhow? Go home. Go home; and let me hear no more of this. And tell the Masther, too, that I'll have to be talkin' to him, if he doesn't keep a guard on his tongue."

I said I balanced accounts with Toal. It was I who, knowing Susie to be smarting under Corney's insults, informed her where her husband was to be found carousing. And in justice to Susie I should say that, had she not been smarting as keenly as she was, she would not have permitted her temper to betray her so.

CHAPTER XVIII.

WHEN GREEK MEETS GREEK.

IT was not till many weeks after the Harvest Fair of Glenties that Ellen Burns learnt the cause of Billy's burst on that day. She found Billy absenting himself from the *Nation*-reading on Sunday afternoons, and, after diligent enquiry, discovered the cause. Then she took an early opportunity of winning his confidence, and establishing herself in his graces once more, by sending Pat the Pedlar to him the next time Pat came around, with the earnest request that Billy would do her the delight of purchasing for her a certain very attractive shawl-pin, the like of which, Pat declared, could not be got this side of Dublin town down of the ridiculous figure for which he offered it—tuppence-ha'penny, to wit. Billy thankfully did Ellen (and equally himself) the delight—after beating Pat down a ha'penny in price, though; and he had the joy of seeing Ellen sport it prominently, and take it out of her shawl, too, for the girls to handle and admire, in Billy's presence, as we all tramped to Mass on the following Sunday. And henceforth Billy was again one of the most eager and constant attendants when Ellen spelled the *Nation*.

But on Easter Sunday afternoon, I remember well, the reading of the *Nation* was for once postponed—as only in the case of a very extraordinary event it ever was, and Ellen was one of the proudest, most hopeful, and most enthusiastic, of the band of partisans who accompanied Billy to the ball-alley on the moor, where, as chosen champion of Knockagar, he was to meet and contest the laurels with Tim Griffin of Glen Ainey. For, at hand ball or at *caman** Billy Brogan was undisputably first among us.

And I well remember, too, how much Billy, whom I had looked up to, rose in my eyes, because of the heroically unostentatious manner in which he bore himself amid the admiration that was showered upon him. Billy's most exalted pleasure, as he went, seemed to be only that he had little Nuala by the hand, and that she beamed upon him, and that Ellen Burns, who went before, linked with the Master, occasionally looked back to

---

* Known in Southern Ireland as hurley

beam upon both of them and to pass a pleasant joke. Beyond his pleasure in this, Billy walked along as if he was a man of no account. I stepped out, alongside Billy and Nuala—for I ever had the craving to keep close to heroes—and my greatest ambition during that evening was to become and to live and die the champion ball player of Knockagar, in succession to Billy Brogan. "Since wishin' is so chape," Corney Higarty said when I had openly expressed my desires, "why wouldn't ye, Dinny, wish at wanst to be the champion ball player of Cork, or Dublin, or Philadelphy, instead of only Knockagar?"

"Because," I replied promptly and earnestly, "it would be far greater and prouder to me to be champion of Knockagar."

Billy looked down on me when I said this, with grateful, happy eyes, in which I almost thought I saw tears spreading. "Dinny," he said, in a quiet tone of voice that was deep with feeling, "Dinny, ye are right there; and them's my feelin's, too."

When Ellen Burns heard what the discussion was about she laughed a quiet laugh, and she said, "Our Dinny is a great dhreamer, entirely: and it has often sthruck me that maybe his dhreams 'll make Knockagar proud of him some day."

I thanked Ellen, who cast back at me a kind,

thoughtful look, with my eyes. Then I shook my head reflectively, and only said, "Ah!"

Tim Griffin and the Glen Ainey boys were just coming streaming over the heather from the North, as we approached the alley (a big bare wall which we had raised in the centre of the moor) from the South. The Glen Ainey boys were fine fellows, and Tim was one of the finest of them—a brave, strapping big fellow, who strode forward with bold pride amid the whole-souled admiration of his fellows. And when I witnessed the boldness of his stride and the confidence of his air my heart sank a little for Billy.

"Billy Brogan," Tim said, as he shook hands with his opponent, "I'm goin' to have the pleasure of givin' ye the biggest dhrubbin' this evenin' that ever ye got in all your born days afore."

"Well, Tim, if ye're the better man, why not?" Billy said, calmly.

Both of them stripped off collar, coat and vest. They laid them in neatly folded heaps on the heather, to one side of the ground, and placed their soft felt hats on top of them. Then they tied their suspenders around their loins and walked into the alley.

The Widow's Pat, as being the most conscientious of men, was unanimously appointed tally-man and judge. He at once marked off the ground, drawing the short-line, the over-all, the dead, and the out; he tossed a *caman* in the air, asking the contestants to call for first hand. Billy called "Bucht up!" and won. Pat then took his position, sitting on a heather hassog to one side of the alley, and marked off the *caman* for a tally-stick; whilst Owen a-Slaivin and John Burns and Toal a-Gallagher and Matthew McCourt, who were all there, took seats around him, to lend him their council on knotty points and to watch the tally.

The Knockagar boys cheered Billy Brogan when he stepped up to the wall and swept the hopping stone with his foot. And the Glen Ainey boys (who had mighty lungs) gave a deafening cheer for Tim Griffin in reply.

"For the glory of Knockagar, Billy, mind," Corney Higarty cried.

"For the glory of Knockagar, Corney, aye," Billy responded.

And then he gave out the first ball, which Tim Griffin instantly killed with such a swift and deadly rooter, that the courage of the Knockagar boys got its first damping, and the Glen Ainey boys cheered jubilantly.

Tim stalked in to take his hand, and to our further dismay, he was soon singing out (and the Glen Ainey boys every one helping him) "Tally wan!" "Tally wan!" and again "Tally wan!" and after another few minutes exciting in-play, " Tally wan!" yet again, and another " Tally wan!"

"Fust five till nought!" Pat doing his stern duty, now cried out in a voice from which, as an impartial official, he nearly succeeded in repressing all traces of the emotion that possessed him.

And then the Glen Ainey boys cheered again. And when, on the heels of this, the Glen Ainey lads joined Tim in another vociferous "Tally wan!" Corney Higarty jumped up from where he had been sitting in mortified silence, behind Pat—Corney, I say sprang up, and with his eye flashing the fire of righteous indignation, yelled at the Glen Ainey boys, "I'll tell yous what it is! Yous is confusin' and dhrivin' distracted the poor boy who's doin' his best to tally this game corract"—and with dramatic gesture he drew the attention of the multitude to "the poor boy," who had on his countenance a look of innocent amazement.

"Right ye are!" said the Vagabone, mounting on a hassog, that he might the better assert him.

"Corney, Corney," Pat pleaded in a pacificatory voice, "They aren't confusin' me."

"But I tell ye they are!" Corney said, with intensified exasperation. "I know better."

"They are," asserted the Vagabone. "The cut-throats!"

Pat heaved a subdued sigh, and concentrated his attention on the blunt edge of his marking-knife.

"Wan 'ud think," Corney said, addressing himself again to the general public, "that its a *newins** for the Glen Ainey boys to get an ace, they guldher so. And now," he said, solemnly, "I want it to be understood that the nixt man or boy opens his jaws for a yell atween this and the finish of the game, he must be prepared to get a cracked neck from me. That's all," he said, and subsided on his heather hassog.

"And to get a drink of his own teeth from me," the Vagabone added.

The Glen Ainey boys, having well interpreted Corney's resolve, were duly demure when, now, he had finished.

During this lull in the game Nuala had gone within the lines, and taken poor Billy by the hand, and spoken cheery words to him; for she felt he needed them. And I had gone in, and walked all around Tim Griffin—who stood like a statue, with arms folded and head at a proud tilt—walked all around him, and viewed him up and down, and said to myself that, surely, poor Billy shouldn't have been expected to beat such a great, well-built fellow. Then I joined Billy and Nuala, and,

---

*A novelty.

meaning to be kind, I said resignedly, "Well, Billy, it'll be small shame to be baiten by Tim Griffin."

"Go away," said Nuala, giving me a push with her disengaged hand, "Billy 'ill not be beaten." But her very anger at the suggestion betrayed her own shaken faith.

"Dinny," Billy said, "don't mind that run of ill-luck. It'll maybe turn. And moreover, if Tim Griffin was as big as a bull and as sthrong, he's not a hair wirier nor me. Never say die, Dinny. 'Tis for the honour of Knockagar." Nuala, overjoyed for the new hope he gave her, clung to his hand with both of hers, and looked up into Billy's mild eyes with tears of gratitude in her own. And I walked out and took my seat at Ellen Burns' feet, and confided in her that I believed Billy would win. And when next Billy looked her way I was rejoiced to see her give him a smile and nod of warm encouragement that made Billy stiffen his back with fresh resolve.

"First five till nought—Go ahead with the game, boys! yous is both doin' finely," Pat now called out. And Tim Griffin strode to the hopping-stone again.

Billy killed the ball next instant with as neat a a rooter as Tim had put in erstwhile, and he proceeded to take his hand. After several minutes' sharp play, Pat, to our delight, sang out: "Boordy five!" and in another minute, "Laidin' ball!" for Billy.

Corney, who had been fidgetty, jumped up in his place at this, and cried out, "A cheer for Billy Brogan and Knockagar!" and got a response with all their hearts, and with all their lungs, from the Knockagar boys.

The Glen Ainey lads grumbled loudly at the flagrant injustice—as they reckoned it—of the autocratic Corney Higarty. But Corney never thought of them or of injustice.

And since the same occasion to be depressed did not then exist, Corney displayed his liberality by raising no angry voice when, Tim Griffin's tally having tardily crept after Billy's, Pat announced "Boordy twelve!" the Glen Ainey boys relieved their feelings with a triumphing cheer.

Henceforward the game grew closer, Billy took the lead with First Fifteen; and by great striving still held it at Look Blunt, Look Sharp, and First Set—when which last was announced we cheered again.

But it was the Glen Ainey boy's turn, when Pat cried "Aboord at First Set!"

"Will ye set it?" asked Tim.

"Don't set it, Billy," cried the impatient Corney.

"Don't set it, Billy," cried Owen a-Slaivin.

"Set it, Billy, by all manner of mains," said the more judicious Toal.

"Set it, William," urged the Master and John Burns, with one voice.

"A sthraight fight, Billy, and no set," shouted the Vagabone.

"I set it," said Billy, "till eleven aces.—Corney," said he, "It's better be ca'tious; and I've got the last* in me, don't you fear."

Every one breathed a deep breath. The Widow's Pat turned over his tally-stick and opened a new account. And the players took their places.

Tim Griffin, who in playing the set seemed to be drawing from latent resources of activity for which we were not prepared, literally ran away with Billy until seven were recorded for him. For, each time of many on which Billy won a hand he walked in and walked out again without as much as one tally. We were very, very much depressed, so when Pat in a weak voice announced "Look Blunt!" the Glen Ainey boys, in the most jubilant of spirits, cheered. Corney's fierce look, as he jumped up again, cut the cheer shorter than it would have been.

"I thought I sayed yous weren't to disthract the boy that's tallyin" indicating Pat, with his hand, "with your yellin' and squealin' like wile boars

---

* The endurance.

a-stickin'. I sayed afore, and I repait to yous now, that the nixt man guldhers, till this game is done and finished, I'll thraw his neck for him."

"And I'll help ye, if ye need it," Owen a-Slaivin said, as warmly as Corney.

"And I'll help ye, too, whether ye need it or not," spoke out the Vagabone.

None of the Glen Ainey boys cared to risk a remonstrance; discretion was, in their estimation, just then, the better part of valour.

But the luck had turned in Billy's favour while yet Corney spoke. He made strokes and turns that caused even the Glen Ainey boys to marvel audibly; and at every fresh feat we said: "Well done, Billy!" and "Brave boy, Billy!" and the Master said, "Bravissimo, William!"

"Second five till Luk Blunt!" Pat, to our delight, soon cried out; and after another ten minutes' highly exciting play, "Aboord at Luk Sharp!" whereupon Corney Higarty and Owen a-Slaivin arose to their feet and led a thunderous cheer.

"That's action for them, Billy! That's play for them!" said Corney then, proudly.

In the next two aces Tim Griffin, with violent effort, led, and when Billy's laurels had seemed in imminent peril "Aboordy Second Set!" was called by Pat.

And then both sides cheered; for they acknowledged that it was a plucky game, and a pretty one, and most excitingly close and well contested.

"I set it to five aces," Tim Griffin announced. And once more we drew a deep breath, and Pat turned his tally-stick.

"Whosomiver wins," said Pat, "needn't cry for shame, anyhow."

"They needn't. They needn't," many voices chorussed.

Whilst the contestants stood in their places for a few minutes to draw breath, Nuala crept over beside me, where I sat entranced, and she whispered, "Dinny, I'm prayin' for Billy. Are you?"

"N—no," I said a little bit shamefacedly.

"Will ye say three Pater-an'-Aves into yerself, now then, Dinny?"

I began to feel a little foolish. I should not like to hurt Nuala by a refusal. And I felt it would be both unmanly and unsportsmanlike to consent.

"Dinny, say ye will," she whispered.

"Well, I will," I said half ungraciously.

And as I rattled through the three Pater-and-Aves, with my thoughts upon the ball-alley, I fear, rather than Heaven, I noticed Nuala whisper something in Ellen's ear, for which Ellen, seizing hold of her, kissed her. She next whispered hurriedly to the Master, who smiled and said,

"Assuredly, Yellow Head, if you vouchsafe me also an osculation." But Nuala only wagged a minatory finger at him, and went on with her message to Pat, who, when he heard it, took on a more solemn look than usual, and patted her approvingly on the head. Toal a-Gallagher looked grave at her whispered request, and gave her an acquiescing nod; whilst Corney Higarty and Owen a-Slaivin both laughed quietly and nodded their heads many times in assurance.

The set of five aces that now started was, according to expectations, the most exciting, and most strenuously contested portion of all the game. But our Billy took the lead and held it till Second Set, where Tim Griffin once again, amid sensational excitement, "boorded" him.

Billy refused to set it. "Do or die, go ahead, Tim Griffin," he said.

Tim gave out what we thought with pain might be the final ball. Billy returned it with great force. Tim turned it again. Billy turned it. Tim turned it by a feat that all there applauded, but did not recover himself after an overreach quickly enough, and lost the hand.

Billy marched up to the hopping-stone without betraying the smallest sign of the nervousness which held all of us, his friends, and which, we felt full sure, must possess him in still greater degree.

He hopped and sent out the ball. Tim, aiming to kill it by a rooter, shot it back with the directness of a bullet from a gun—every man had unconsciously risen to his feet and craned his neck—it struck—the ground, just one bare inch from the root of the wall!

The fight was fought and won. The day was Knockagar's and Billy's!

And when Corney Higarty led the cheer that was both loud and ringing, even the Glen Ainey boys themselves joined.

CHAPTER XIX.

AFTER THE BATTLE.

BILLY BROGAN was wringing Tim Griffin's hand, where the two stood within the lines, and assuring him that he, Tim, was a prince among players. Corney, when he had finished his cheer, stepped in, and, taking Tim's hand in both of his, wrung it with right good will. "Tim Griffin," said he, still shaking Tim's hand, but speaking at the crowd, "I feel it an honour to be allowed to grip the hand of ye. Ye're a credit to Glen Ainey and a credit to the County Donegal. Ye're a gintleman and a ball player.—Boys," said he, dropping Tim's hand, "give us three cheers from the bottom of your stomachs for Tim Griffin, the best ball player on Ireland's groun' bar wan; and for the Glen Ainey boys, the best jintlemen in Irelan' bar none, and mannerly conducted."

And though the Knockagar boys answered

Corney's appeal with a heart and a half, none there responded with more alacrity or lung power than the Glen Ainey boys themselves.

"Boys," said Tim Griffin then, "I consider it an honour to be baiten by Misther Brogan," indicating, with a dramatic wave of his hand, the violently blushing Billy; for Billy was pleasingly confused by the sudden access of honour, having never been styled Misther in his life before, except on the (still preserved) envelope of a letter which a lawyer in Philadelphia (who, of course, did not know him) had written him a year before, saying that his uncle Taig was nearing death, and was old and childless, and asking to be employed to look after Billy's interests.

It is hard to say whether Tim or Billy was congratulated most; but I know that Billy drew the most worship—worship that was not the less sincere because most of it was silent.

Though Nuala had penetrated the crowd and kept Billy by the hand throughout the congratulatory commotion, Ellen remained outside his ring of worshippers until, the excitement having subsided, he, with Nuala, made his way out. Then Ellen bestowed a smile on him that, momentary though it was, almost outweighed all the glory of the evening gone before.

And then, guarded by Nuala and Ellen, Billy, his

heart bathed in happiness, started over the moor for home. And the Knockagar boys all streamed after.

"Dionysius, my lad," said the Master, stepping up alongside me, where I had walked alone, following at a distance the footsteps of the three— "Dionysius, my lad, when heroes are on the heath, nonentities like yourself and my more humble self, are temporarily consigned to oblivion."

I asked, "What do ye mean, Masther?"

"Dionysius," he said, shaking a rebuking finger at me, "do not deny that you were grieving just now. Ellen and Nuala considered themselves honoured in being permitted to pedestrianise with us only one hour gone. Now they have got a hero and forgotten us."

I said: "I'm not vexed, Masther. I'm glad Billy is a hero, and that Nuala and Ellen are so good to him; and I'm so proud he is a hero, that for thinkin' of him I had forgot meself; little wonder, then, any one else should forget me."

The Master laid his hand on my head for a moment, and he then patted me on the back, gently.

"Dionysius," he said, after a minute, "has it discovered itself to you that you are a little hero?"

"I'm no hero; and never was one; and ye need not make fun of me, Masther," I said. "But I know I'd like to try all me life to be a hero like Billy Brogan."

"And your denial finally demonstrates that you are what you believe yourself to be not," said the Master.

I made no reply, for I could not understand him.

The moor was what Billy called haggary walking for Nuala, so he, after awhile, insisted that she must get upon his back, to effect which he stood her upon a hassog, and hunkered low himself. He caught her arms around his neck and put each of her feet into a capacious side-pocket of his jacket. When Nuala was mounted she looked around and laughed to us, half shame-facedly, and wholly pleased. I smiled a pleased smile, and nodded my head to signify my approval. "Yellow-Head, Yellow-Head," the Master said, shaking his fist toward her, "without doing half so much to merit it, you have risen superior to the hero." The Master's manner put Nuala more at her ease, and she rang out one of her own little silvery laughs.

When, Knockagar being reached, the party broke up, Billy walked with me toward my own home on the hill. For, curiously, Billy found in youngsters rather than in men his congenial companions. Me in particular he favoured. I said:

"Billy, you're a proud man this night."

"In throth, Dinny," he said, "I can't well tell ye

whither I am or no." And he smiled an apologetic smile for his ignorance.

"And a happy man, too," I said.

"Happy? I'm that, yis. Aye, I'm that."

"Ellen was very good to you the day, Billy," said I.

"Ellen?" Billy said. "Ellen couldn't be other than good if she tried. God bliss her!"

Then Billy grew reflective; and I respected his mood for several minutes. Though I loved the Masther, I sympathized more deeply with Billy, and so wished to think that Billy might yet have a chance of winning Ellen. So, after a while I broke the silence, saying:

"There's one thing I wisht with all me heart."

"What's that, chile?" Billy asked.

"I wisht that Ellen Burns 'ud marry you, Billy."

Billy shook his head slowly and gravely.

"Dinny, chile," said he, "it's good of ye. But you'll never see it."

"And why?"

"Bekase,"* he replied, sententiously.

"Bekase what?" I asked.

"Dinny, Ellen Burns is far-and-away beyont me."

"Ellen Burns," I said, "is far-and-away beyont everybody in the wurrl', for that part of it."

* Because, *i.e.* for very sufficient reason.

"Right!" said Billy, "Right!"

"But sure she must marry some of them, all the same; and she'll marry the best."

"Exactly," said Billy. "And what else could be expected of her? And that's the raison that I've long since seen it foolish of the likes of me to even think of the likes of Ellen Burns." After a few moments he said, in a burst, "But, Dinny, I just couldn't help bein' in love with her, no matter how much I tried—I don't know how it was," he said, shaking his head puzzledly.

"It was all natural," I said. "Sure I was bad in love with Ellen meself till I seen the foolishness of me thinkin' of the likes of Ellen."

"I wisht," said Billy, heaving a sigh, "I could see the foolishness of it meself. For it was surely foolishness of me."

"If, as you say, Ellen marries the best, Billy," I said emphatically, "then she must marry you."

"Thanky, thanky," Billy said, with a tolerant smile. "But that'll be the Masther. And it's him she'll marry."

I could not answer this last assertion; for my own observation forced me, against my wish, to the some conclusion.

"But, Dinny," he said in a cheery tone, "it's the Masther that's desarvin' of her, and it's her that's desarvin' of him. And I wish, from me sowl, God to prosper and bliss them both—if, as I think, it comes to that atween them. I've a sort of made up me mind, Dinny, that poor Billy hasn't (and shouldn't expect) any chance. Ever since thon Harwist Fair of Glentics, I've been thryin' to make up me mind, and I think, with God's help, I'll soon have it done. *Beannacht leat,* Dinny, *a theagair! Beannacht leat!*"

I said "*Coimrigh 'n Righ leat,** Billy." And I stood gazing after him, and listening as he went down the hill in the moonlight, singing:

"Och Erin's Isle, this soul of mine it longs to see ye free;
Where'er I wander sure this heart it burns and baits for thee;
I'm grieved to see thee so oppressed; but what can I do more?
Och, Gramochree, I weep for thee—Old Irelan' I adore!"

"Poor Billy!" I muttered. And my heart was sad for him as I turned and went into the house.

---

* The protection of The King (*i.e.* God) with thee.

CHAPTER XX.

INTELLECTUAL FEATS BY THE FIRESIDE AND ELSEWHERE.

As the *Bacach Fada*, or Tall Beggarman, had invited himself to lodge, on a night, with the Widow's Pat, the neighbours foregathered there also, to hear from the Beggarman's lips the news of the world, and the world's anticipations and expectations. For, the *Bacach Fada* had ever some strange and startling intelligence of happenings in the outer world—intelligence which he had gleaned by bits and scraps from all sorts of people and from all corners of the County Donegal.

Of course any Beggarman had the right to walk in and make himself at home—for a night or for a week—in any house he chose, everywhere he went. But when, in their wanderings, they reached Knockagar, the beggarmen had a singular fancy for imposing themselves on Pat's easy good-nature, so that, as Corney Higarty put it, "'Tis seldom but me frien' Pat is bliss'd with a good beggarman in his corner."

The house at which the *Bacach Fada* deigned to drop his bags was in the *Bacach Fada's* opinion done a signal honour. "And bekase I esteem me frien' Pathrick far above the or'nary," he would say, "that is why I am so partial to his humble cabin." And, indeed, Pat felt the honour of entertaining this autocrat, to whom all the country looked up, and who in turn looked down with tolerant contempt upon all the country.

Billy Brogan called for me, saying that the *Bacach Fada* was in Pat's, and that as Corney Higarty had gone up, "there'll be some enthertainin' goin's-on." So Billy and I walked there together.

The Autocrat had monopolized for himself and his legs the cosiest chimney corner. His half-a-dozen wallets were piled behind him, and his oaken cudgel lay on top of them. The respectful neighbours were seated wherever they could. He had finished "puttin' Nuala through her facin's on the school-books," and, to Pat's great pride, had vouchsafed that she was "modherately passable—modherately passable." Seeing me enter, he thought he had hold of a still better subject upon whom to air his vanity. "Progress hitherwards,

Denis O'Friel," he said, "till I invistigate your pretensions, and demonsthrate and castigate your laxity of intellectuality."

"Indeed, and I'll do no such a thing, *Bacach*," I said, with a boldness that electrified the neighbours. But I had often longed to rebel against the tyrannical yoke which this fellow had laid upon the minds of men.

Every one looked at me in horror.

"And for why, Dinny, chile, 'ont ye let the *Bacach Fada* cross-quistion ye upon your lessons?" Pat asked.

I said, "Because it's only fool questions without either rhyme or raison he puts on me."

"Right," said Corney Higarty, who was an iconoclast. "A man who was born and bred in a schoolhouse, and fed upon dixonaries, couldn't answer his queskins."

The neighbours felt that they were much outraged in Corney, who had not even my excuse of immaturity to palliate his offence against the sacred person of the *Bacach*.

I was mentally very, very grateful to Corney. At Ned McCool's wake, only ten nights before, the *Bacach Fada*, casting around him for some peg on which to hang his vanity, had alighted upon me, and mortified me deeply by starting me—with the whole wakehouse attending eagerly—such questions as, "How could you demonsthrate the South and circular sides of a three-year oul' whinstone by the square and kibe roots of jo-omethry and thrigonomethry?" and "Could you state paragorically the number of faddoms of wind that blows through the chancel window of Donegal oul' Abbey in the month of March, and prove the same by Vulgar Fractions and the rule of Double Position?" Although I had previously passed, in the neighbours' eyes, for "a smart, cliver young fella," they shook their heads over my failure to answer these, and said both myself and my masther might be clever enough in our own way, "but the *Bacach Fada*, who never darkened a school doore but three times in his life, can give the pair o' them points yet."

"Cornelius Higarty," the beggarman said, "I blame you not. Your profession as an itinerant disciple of Mars is your all sufficin' excuse for lacking the appreciation of the spiritual and intellectual arts."

"Are ye insinuatin' anything, me frien'?" Corney asked with a warlike light rekindling in his eye.

"I only say," replied the *Bacach*, who never could tyrannise over Corney, "that a veth'ran warrior is not supposed to be acquainted with the intellectual attainments that a poor scholar like myself humbly prides himself upon."

"Blatheration! And thanky for nothin'," said

Corney, shortly. "If ye'd dhrop in to my wee cabin of an evenin' when Dinny here, and Nuala and the Vagabone, and all the other youngsters (and in faith some of the oldsthers, too, the Widow's Pat, there, and Billy Brogan); if ye were in my little hut of a cabin, I say, when these come in and bother me till I give them out some of me puzzles, ye'd sing very small entirely about your intellectial entertainments."

"Right ye are, Corney," spoke up Billy Brogan, daring in a good cause to be bold.

And I, too, said, "Right ye are, Corney."

"Just as a speciment, Corney," Billy asked, "give us wan of your delightful puzzles."

Nuala and I drew forward eagerly. Even Pat rubbed his hands and said, "Do, Corney. Do, Corney."

"To oblige me good and valued friends William and Pathrick, I will," said Corney. "Which will it be?"

"'The King sent his Lady,' keepin' your breath in," said Billy enthusiastically.

"'All-a-long, all-a-long, you,'" said Pat, as enthusiastically.

"Then it'll be both—with a heart and a half," said Corney.

All hitched their chairs and rearranged themselves.

"Each varse of this, from the first small wan till the last long one, and the last long wan as well as the first small wan, must be sayed complete—and ye may say it as fast as it plaises ye—without dhrawin' a new breath—I call this puzzle

"'THE KING SENT HIS LADY.

"'The King sent his lady, on the first fine day,
A parthridge, a parrot—so now let me see
Who'll l'arn this carol that carries from me.'"

"That's wan breath," Corney said. "The nixt is—

"'The King sent his lady on the nixt fine day
Two starlings, a parthridge, a parrot, so now let me see
Who'll l'arn this carol that carries from me.'"

"That's wan breath, too."

"Baithershin!" the *Bacach Fada* contemptuously ejaculated.

The Widow's Pat and Billy ably supported Corney in looking daggers at the fellow, as Corney proceeded with the next part.

"'The King sent his lady on the third fine day
Three gold rings, two starlings, a parthridge—a parrot, and
now let me see
Who'll l'arn this carol that carries from me.'"

"And you just wait, *Bacach Fada*, till I'm finished afore ye say 'Baithershin!'"

"Aye!" said Pat. And, "Let him!" said Billy: and he added, "I'll give him a scon if he's fit to say it."

"'The King sent his lady on the fourth fine day,'"

Corney went on—

"'Four geese that was grey,
Three gold rings, two starlings, a parthridge, a parrot—and now let me see
Who'll l'arn this carol that carries from me.'"

"Very good," Corney said, in self-approval. And went on again—

"'The King sent his lady on the fiff' fine day
Five swans a-merry swimming, four geese that was grey,
Three gold rings, two starlings, a parthridge, a parrot—and now let me see
Who'll l'arn this carol that carries from me.'"

"'Tis well ye do it, Corney!" Pat encouraged him. And, "Well! Well!" Billy Brogan repeated. Corney fixed the *Bacach Fada* with his eye as he began the next—

"'The King sent his lady on the six' fine day
Six crowns a-merry coddling, five swans a-merry swimming, four geese that was grey,
Three gold rings, two starlings, a parthridge, a parrot—and now let me see
Who'll l'arn this carol that carries from me.'"

"Hagh!" Billy ejaculated at the *Bacach Fada.* Corney went on—

"'The King sent his lady on the seventh fine day
Seven hounds a-merry hunting, six crowns a-merry coddling,
five swans a-merry swimming, four geese that was grey,
Three gold rings, two starlings, a parthridge, a parrot—and
now let me see
Who'll l'arn this carol that carries from me.'"

"'The King sent his lady on the eighth fine day
Eight bulls that was brown,
Seven hounds a-merry hunting, six crowns a-merry coddling,
five swans a-merry swimming, four geese that was grey,
Three gold rings, two starlings, a parthridge, a parrot—and
now let me see
Who'll l'arn this carol that carries from me.'"

"'The King sent his lady on the ninth fine day
Nine bucks a-merry bounding, eight bulls that was brown,
Seven hounds a-merry hunting, six crowns a-merry coddling,
five swans a-merry swimming, four geese that was grey,
Three gold rings, two starlings, a parthridge, a parrot—and
now let me see
Who'll l'arn this carol that carries from me.'"

"Are ye listenin' to that *Bacach?*" Pat asked, triumphing.

But there was really little need to ask: the *Bacach Fada* was listening earnestly, a serious look, quick growing to gravity, had replaced on his countenance, the contemptuous look with which he had greeted Corney's beautiful puzzle.

"And, *Bacach*, that isn't the whole of it," Billy Brogan said.

Corney, who scorned any unfair device for regaining his wind, waited not—

"'The King sent his lady on the tenth fine day
Ten maids a-merry meeting, nine bucks a-merry bounding eight bulls that were brown,
Seven hounds a-merry hunting, six crowns a-merry coddling, five swans a-merry swimming, four geese that was grey,
Three gold rings, two starlings, a parthridge, a parrot—and now let me see
Who'll l'arn this carol that carries from me.'"

To the intense admiration of all, and the proud delight of three, this last extraordinary effort reddened Corney's face considerably. We looked on him as a Roman audience must have looked long since, on a sorely tried but resolute gladiator. Corney wiped from his brow the beads of perspiration; we looked at the *Bacach Fada*, now growing shame-faced; and Corney again took up his now huge task—

"'The King sent his lady on the 'leventh fine day
Eleven lads a-merry larking, ten maids a-merry meeting, nine bucks a-merry bounding, eight bulls that were brown,
Seven hounds a-merry hunting, six crowns a-merry coddling, five swans a-merry swimming, four geese that was grey,
Three gold rings, two starlings, a parthridge, a parrot—and now let me see
Who'll l'arn this carol that carries from me.'"

"Good ye do it, Corney!" "Good!" "Good!" all encouraged him. And he essayed the last part of the task—

"'The King sent his lady on the twel'th fine day
Twelve bishops was blue,
Eleven lads a-merry larking, ten maids a-merry meeting, nine
bucks a-merry bounding, eight bulls that was brown,
Seven hounds a-merry hunting, six crowns a-merry coddling,
five swans a-merry swimming, four geese that was grey,
Three gold rings, two starlings, a parthridge, a parrot—and
now let me see ,
Who's l'arnt this carol that carried from me.'"

Corney was very red in the face now; but he had triumphed. Billy Brogan, advancing, clapped him on the back, at the same time turning a defiant eye upon the discomfited *Bacach Fada*. Pat's gaze, beaming with delight, roamed over every countenance visible in the firelight, collecting Corney's tribute. And he got a goodly store. As his joy was never complete till he had induced all the world to share it with him, so also his pride. He saw that every one there—the *Bacach Fada* only excepted—was now as proud as he himself was of his hero; so he was satisfied.

"*Bacach Fada*," Billy Brogan said, "will ye thry that puzzle, and prove your smartness to these people?"

But the *Bacach* replied promptly. "As it is no

intellectial fait, I disdain to thry it—though I could perform it as aisy as turn on me heel."

"But I say it is an intellectial fait," Billy Brogan, with the very vaguest idea of what an intellectual feat meant, positively asseverated.

"If an intellectial fait mains an extraor'inary one," Pat said, "I would say it's the intellectialest fait I've ever witnessed."

"And besides," Billy Brogan continued to the *Bacach*, "ye couldn't do it no more nor ye could go over the moon with a stannin' jump."

"As ye have shuparior advantage of me in age," said the *Bacach*, sarcastically, "I'll not call ye a liar."

"Thanky," Billy said. "Corney," he went on, "just to show him another intellectial fait, give us 'All-a-long, all-a-long, you.'"

"Yis," said Pat, enthusiastically, "give us 'All-a-long,' Corney, please."

"Clear the hearth-stone," said Corney. And immediately several hands were busy clearing and cleaning it; when which was done, Corney, getting upon his knees, and taking in his fingers a bit of chalk, repeated the "All-a-long" rhyme at a breathless rate, at the same time making, as fast as he could, and uncalculatingly as it seemed, a row of chalk-strokes upon the clean flag—the first stroke going down with the first word, and the last stroke with the last word, to our mystification, admiration, and wonder contriving to have not one stroke less or more than 32 at the finish, Corney said:

"All-a-long, all-a-long, all-a-long, you,
Mirry-go-round, lantern blue,
Jaramy, aramy, black-foot man
Thirteen and nineteen makes twenty-wan
Heather-skite, blether-skite, amadan, fool,
I went three wet days to a tinker's school,
But I'll widger ten guineas with any of you
There isn't wan there but thirty and two."

/ /

There they were, rapid and unreckoning as he put them down, thirty-two strokes exactly, just as he asserted. The Widow's Pat counted them. Billy Brogan counted them, several of the neighbours counted them in turn. And thirty-two they, one and all, made them out.

Pat was proud, Billy defiant, the neighbours amazed, the *Bacach Fada* supercilious, and Corney Higarty unconcerned as any true hero.

Oft had Pat tried the "All-a-long" puzzle, and almost as often had he failed. The number of his strokes, when reckoned in cold blood, generally totted up in the neighbourhood of forty-nine. On one memorable occasion, indeed, his marks came out thirty-two exactly; and Toal a-Gallagher endeavoured to cloud Pat's glory saying that Micky Hude's cow killed a hare once, by tramping on it. Toal added that though Micky's cow lived to a venerable age she never killed another. Pat, too, never hit the thirty-two mark again. Billy Brogan had also attempted the puzzle many a time and oft, but, like Pat, having never discovered that the secret lay in reckoning with the rhythmic feet, he met with little better success than his friend.

"*Bacach,*" Billy Brogan now said, "what do ye think?"

"I think," the Bacach said as he arose, "it is time I partook of my frugial supper." For, in the excitement created by Corney's intellectual feats, he almost forgot a big plate of stirabout which he had laid to cool on the thornbush at the side of the house.

The *Bacach Fada* went out of doors, and, a minute later, returned with deliberate stride, holding in his hand an emptied plate.

"Since the wurrl' was created in the book of Ginesis," he said angrily, holding forward for our inspection the plate, "was such a rasky-ality ever sartified to?"

"What is it?" said Pat, who, to his pain, more than dimly guessed the truth.

"The supper," said the *Bacach Fada,* shaking the emptied plate at arm's length with indignant gesture. "The frugal supper of the homeless and the orphan vilely absthracted from off the plate on the bush without your doore."

Said Owen a-Slaivin, "As I come in, I noticed the Vagabone and two or three more scoundhrels lyin' about the ditches."

"The Vagabone then it was, sure enough," said Pat, shaking his head, resignedly. And the neighbours said, "The Vagabone it was then, och-och!"

The *Bacach Fada* said bitterly, "It was the Vagabone. And may he meet his daith by suspinsion."

Corney Higarty was eyeing the dimensions of the plate narrowly. "If the Vagabone, with no more help than from two or three more scoundhrels, ate the contents of that plate of stirabout, it is what I call an intellectial fait for which he desarves, and gets from me, the heighth of credit."

It was the severely sour aspect of the *Bacach Fada* only, which compelled the neighbours to enjoy Corney's remark in the secrecy each of his own bosom.

CHAPTER XXI.

THE PILGRIMAGE TO LOCH DEARG.

On a beautiful day in early June a little band of pilgrims went south on the road from Knockagar. The destination was to be St. Patrick's Purgatory on wild Loch Dearg. The organizer, director and father of the little band was the Widow's Pat, whose eye was that day more than usually softened by the look of grave reflection and saintly humility which, appropriate to such occasion, held it. As the pilgrim band went out of Knockagar Pat walked by the donkey's head. On the cart he had fastened his turf-cadgings, and on a litter of heather and dried grass within squatted Ellen Burns, Nuala, and myself. Toal a-Gallagher, with solemn demeanor, walked alongside the cart, and the Master and Billy Brogan, marching, smilingly, at the tail of the cart, brought up the rear of a little procession—a cavalcade, Corney Higarty dubbed it—which attracted no little attention and created no little excitement in Knockagar.

I said that Pat—who was always a sort of lay missionary amongst us—was the organizer of the expedition. Of the many pilgrim bands that, every summer, journeyed from Knockagar for three days' prayer and mortification at the famous Purgatory of Loch Dearg, the Widow's Pat always got together, and conveyed, one, and that not the least important. He was this year short of Susie Gallagher, who had always joined his penitent party. Susie, in her heart, could never quite bring herself to forgive the Master for his heinous conduct in miscalling her a troglodyte, and when Pat pressed her to join the party, she refused on the ground that her prayers in that man's company would do her harm rather than good. This time, as on previous occasions, all Pat's eloquence could not induce his friend Corney—for whose spiritual welfare he was painfully solicitous—to make the pilgrimage. Pat came away from his interview very grave indeed, for Corney, in reply to his solicitations, had assured him that he was "feelin' too oul' to join pleasure parties."

So often and so much had I heard of the penitential island in Loch Dearg that, apart altogether from my religious inclinations in the matter—and they were strong—it was a joy to me when my Uncle Donal consented to my going. I had come to the time to be responsible for my own soul, Pat impressed my Uncle. "And little Nuala, is likewise; so I'm fetchin' her, too," Pat said. And, indeed, I had, myself, begun to feel of late that sense of independent individuality which heralds incipient manhood; and my years, now sixteen, warranted the conclusion, methought. Nuala and myself were mutually rejoiced to find that we were to accompany each other. For latterly, we had been much together, our sympathies and our tastes growing daily more akin, and daily making of us warmer friends and closer comrades.

Barring our journey to the Glenties Harvest Fair, now nearly two years ago, and her first journey hither, this was our first expedition into the unknown.

We were now to cross the far distant range of purple hills that had been my awe in childhood and a source of wonder to me ever since—and to Nuala as well. For, often and often, when she kept me company in lone Glenboran, had we sat with our eyes riveted long on that line of hills on which the sky leant, and speculated regarding the feelings of those who lived beneath their shadows, the sensations of those who trod them, and the wonders disclosed to those who reached their crests and gazed upon the strange new world which lay beyond. And now at length our curiosity was to be gratified and our speculation set at rest.

After five or six hours' travelling through a land of ever-fresh delights—for, everything that differed from what we had been used to see at Knockagar was to us a delight—we reached the last cabin at the end of the last bye-road, the limit as it seemed of civilization; and here we three descended from off the cart. The donkey was unharnessed, and stalled in the byre of the hospitable good man who resided at this outpost of humanity, and while Ellen prepared a meal (the materials for which we had brought with us), Billy Brogan, and Nuala, and I took observation of the country, pleasantly surprised to find the little cabins, far away from the world though we thought them, neat, and white, and trig, and comfortable, and the people looking as cheery and merry as even the inhabitants of Knockagar. After closely questioning several people whose looks spake surprise that any one should question their happiness, I was still in my heart of hearts unconvinced that they could be as content as they seemed. And Billy Brogan agreed with me; though Nuala would not.

"How could these people be happy, Billy," I said, as we sat philosophising on a clay ditch, "when they haven't got (as they couldn't, of course, have) any place to go at night as entertainin' as Toal's?"

"Ay? Ay?" Billy said, shaking his head reflectively.

"Or any man as entertainin' as Toal himself?" I said.

"Or any such an intherestin' man as John Burns?" Billy said. "Or such a l'arned man as the Masther?"

"Or how can they even live without Corney Higarty amongst them?" said I.

"Or Owen a-Slaivin?" Billy said triumphantly, "Or a girl like Ellen.—Or like Nuala here," he added quickly, remembering himself. "It's my opinion," Billy went on decisively, "that that black-avised man that laughed when you axed him if he was railly happy—it's my opinion that that fella is what Corney Higarty calls a hipplecrit."

Ellen here called us in to our meal, putting a close to the discussion just then; though Billy and I often took it up again in after days, striving hard to confirm each other in the prejudice that true happiness was utterly impossible in the fringes of the world beyond the social radius of Knockagar.

We made a hearty meal on cappered oatbread, eggs and milk. And after a further rest we bent us to the hills. But first all who wore shoes, which is to say all except Nuala and me, took them off, and, tying the whang ends together, slung them over-shoulder. Billy Brogan insisted on carrying Ellen's boots, which after protestation she let him have. I should have mentioned, too, that Pat left most particular directions about the food and care his donkey was to receive till our return.

As we had left home with the morning, it was still the early afternoon when we began the ascent of the brown hills. Brown those hills were, which to me had hitherto looked purple.

"It's a desaivin' wurrl', faith," Billy said, for he was in a moralizing mood—"Far-away cows have long horns. It's just like what has happened to meself, in a fair, more than wanst; I've often follied (followed) for half-a-day, through the fair, a sprig of a *cailín* that I thought mighty purty lookin', but when I'd at last musther enough desperation to come close and put spake on her—phew! She was as common as three-a-penny. Not," he added, "that these hills is common—but they have their deceptions all the same." That they had; for neither were they by any means so high nor so steep as my childish fancy had pictured. They now looked to be gently rising moorlands, with elevated plateau-passes intersecting the ridge. And when, at length, we reached the highest point, I, in common with Nuala, and with Billy, was not a little disappointed to find that the strange world beyond, instead of bursting on our straining vision, was still shut out by a long stretch of plateau.

Yet, far from my interest flagging, I was fascinated with the sensation of stillness and loneliness, and almost desolation, which these vast tracts of mountain-moor imparted ; and, as I walked, my soul absorbed the sensation greedily as a dry sponge moisture. And when I listed I quit dreaming, and took my place in the journeying group, hearkening to Pat's anecdotes, or the grave discussions which, carried on between Toal and the Master, beguiled the way.

The sun was bearing low in the heavens when we reached the crest of the plateau, and the scene I had longed to witness was suddenly disclosed to my view. But, instead of the new world which my imagination had conjured up, I beheld a great beyond-the-world tract.

The region unveiled below us consisted of many, many miles of brown, brown, wild and monotonous moor, with such little suggestion of the neighbourhood of human-kind that it might well have been a thousand miles from humanity. Except for one incongruous thing. A small island in the middle of a great shining lake which occupied the centre of the scene, seemed crowded to the very water's edge with buildings; and a big black boat, laden with people, was cumbrously crawling over the waters in the direction of the island.

Toal, with a sigh of relief, laid himself down upon

the crest, and the others all sank around him, with eyes rivetted upon the lake—the far-famed Loch Dearg.

"'Tis a gloryus sight!" ejaculated Pat. All felt the full truth of the remark, but no one spoke. The sun was slanting his rays across the scene, turning to slumberous gold the bleak brown of the great moor, and causing the waters of the loch to shimmer and dance as if delighted with his arch caress. He touched with his torch the banks of flowering whins that arose beyond the loch to the left, and they flamed with a fierce intensity that strikingly contrasted with the joyous passiveness of the remainder of the wide scene. One little, white-walled, thatch-bound cabin, too, my eye detected after a time. It was just peeping over the shoulder of a brown knoll, and a thin curl of blue turf smoke was twisting up from its tiny chimney, mounting straight toward the clear sky above. And I saw with my mental eye a clean-swept hearth, chickens hurriedly pecking over the forbidden clay floor, and a white-capped, white-haired, clear-skinned woman spinning by the fireside, and crooning a soft old Gaelic song, broken now and then by an objurgation to the temporarily-frighted chickens.

To Nuala, whom I had seated beside me, I imparted my dream about the suggestive, lone, little cottage; and her eye lighted as I drew the picture.

"Oh!" Nuala said enthusiastically, "that nice old woman must be so happy all by her lone self, or only with the cows and chickens, and her little dog there."

"And she travels far away to some town, maybe once in six weeks," I said, "and gets her groceries, and comes back to her own happiness then, for six weeks more."

"And before she starts for the town," said Nuala, "she takes down her beads from the nail by the fireside where they hang, and she prays on them as she goes and comes over the lone moor."

"Do you know," said Billy Brogan, who had been overhearing our conversation all the time, "Dinny O'Friel has you near a'most as bad as himself, Yalla Head—dhraimin' things, and yous both awake."

Nuala laughed ripplingly, and said, "Ay, it's just Dinny is spoiling me. And I do notice that I'm getting into his way of dreaming things, and me awake."

The Master and Ellen had to be informed of the nature of the discussion.

The Master then said: "William speaks truly. Yellow Head, you will recall the moral headline

I have so often set you, 'Evil communications corrupt good manners?' You would not be warned by it. Dionysius the Dreamer was born to an estate on Mount Parnassus——"

"Where's that?" Billy interrupted interestedly.

"In Greece, William, in Greece."

"Oh—h—h!"

"But the heritage, like that of most poets, is so heavily mortgaged that payment of the interest demands a life-time's strenuous work. Take the advice of a philosopher, little Yellow Head, and for the future be more chary of bestowing your company upon the Poet."

Because her uncle's eyes and Toal's, and Ellen's were bent upon her, a little veil of confusion overspread Nuala's face, as she tried to laugh acknowledgment to the Master's advice. Ellen shifted herself over behind Nuala, threw her arms around her neck and kissed her on the brow. And she said, "Don't mind him, Nuala. Don't mind the Master. He's always—always——"

"Full of his nadiums and antics," poor Billy said, supplying the needed sense.

"Exactly," said Ellen, and kissed Nuala again.

The Master said, "And now, my Lady, tender the balm of Gilead to Dionysius."

But I drew away haughtily, and to the Master's

great enjoyment, looked upon him with severity amounting almost to a frown.

Toal and Pat got to their feet and led the way, now down hill and easy, towards the Loch. The Master and Ellen followed, and Nuala, Billy, and I brought up the rear. My good humour was, under the influence of the glorious evening, soon restored, and I had not hopped over many heather-knowes till I was answering in kind the Master's back-thrown banter.

As we progressed over the heather the sun bent lower and still lower, till at length it sank behind the hills. Then the hitherto shimmering loch, like a thing of life instantly paralysed, became an intensely calm unrippled sea, with, not alone its islands, but the rising moors and the peaks of distant hills mirrored in it. The flaming whins, away to the left, suddenly sobered in their flaunting mood, and gradually dropped the exulting assertiveness with which they had all day long unintermittently flashed their fierce colour above the modest brown of the lovely heather. For a time after the sun had gone from sight a warm-tinted glow still lingered over the great moor as if loath to leave; but it stole away, at length, before the shades that came sifting down, and a dim mystery descended on the hollows and the farther stretches of the moor; whereat, I knew not why or how—and I never have known—a sweet sadness filled my heart, till tears swam in my eyes. The call of a plover, or the cry of a pheasant, at intervals burst the thick stillness that lay over the scene; or again a tinkling sound, or a musical murmur of voices, startled us by seeming to rise at our feet, or come from the nearest knowe—whereas they were carried over the waters from the Station Island.

As we advanced we had gradually ceased speaking, my hand had sought Nuala's and held it, unreluctantly on her part; and so we had trudged forward hand in hand. Reading the soul that looked out through her great wondering eyes, I saw that she was all unconscious of everything save the universal bliss—God's benison—enveloping all earthly things that evening of evenings. Then I began wondering if the spirit of this evening was common to the place, and intended, as now, to enwrap the souls and senses of all who came to the Holy Island to seek close communion with their God; and I anyhow felt it was the most fitting preparation for a holy time of penance and prayer that he could vouchsafe us.

The night-shades had fallen thickly when we reached the Loch shore. We gathered dry heather, and bramble enough to make a signal fire. But as Toal and Pat had rightly surmised, our signal was not answered from the Island (which was about two miles distant); evidently because, as we had come upon the shore at a point far eastward of where the pilgrims usually arrive, our fire was not observed by the Island boatmen. Pat unfolded a bundle of cappered oatbread and divided it among us. All had keen appetites after our long moor tramp, and ate heartily. As we finished our meal, the beautiful strains of a hymn sung by many voices and softened by distance, were wafted o'er the waters to us, and to it, as to a benediction, we hearkened with bowed heads. Anything more strikingly and beautifully impressive than those blissful strains suddenly starting upon the night, and sounding across that lone loch in the midst of a great wild moor, and almost seeming sung for the behoof of the little band of belated penitents who sat upon the shingly shore, I have rarely heard—if ever.

Afterwards, Ellen led in two of the Loch Dearg hymns which she and Pat and Toal and the Master had learnt on previous pilgrimages; and Billy, Nuala, and myself made effort to come in upon an occasional bar. Though Ellen's voice was most musical and Billy's likewise, I fear that Toal and Pat all unconsciously had marred much the general effect in the ear of an unsympathetic audience—yet to us, and on the occasion, even Toal and Pat were almost sublime.

Pat's eyes were welling with tears when he had finished. He turned to Ellen and said, in a voice that was soft, even for him, "Ellen Burns, the Bliss'd Virgin Mary, as she bends down from Heaven now listenin', has pride in her pure heart for ye."

Ellen turned her face away from the dying fire-light. I saw the Master's eyes glinting wet in the flickering glow. Nuala was startled by a sting upon her cheek, and instantly Billy Brogan, who was bending above her, hurriedly and shamefacedly, with his rough hand wiped away a teardrop which had there fallen.

"Let us say the Rosary and retire," said Toal-a-Gallagher, drawing forth his beads.

We all drew out our beads; and we knelt in a circle, some on the shingle, some on the heather, and from our hearts chorussed the responses to Toal, or led, each in turn, in a decade. The Rosary of the Five Joyful Mysteries it was that Toal recited. He needed neither light nor book, for he had all the Rosaries by heart and he worded the Mysteries in an impressive manner, pouring into them the fulness of a pious heart. A belated curlew called lonely from afar, and the faintest little wavelets lapped the shingly shore, as Toal proceeded, and an occasional murmur, too, was wafted to us over the water from the Holy Isle. The volume of our own voices, when we murmurously responded, filled the air so that it seemed as if a multitude prayed upon the moor. Such joyous bliss, too, filled our souls as if we waited outside the gate, on the eve of our entrance into Paradise.

At the conclusion of the Rosary, Toal asked one Pater-and-Ave for the benefit of all the pilgrims now on the Island, and for all that had ever been on it, and for all to come henceforth, that God might give them the reward they sought; one Pater-and-Ave for God to look with favour on our own little pilgrimage, and grant us His grace to make it a stepping-stone to Eternal bliss; and a Pater-and-Ave (which was meant for Billy, and which Toal never overlooked at the end of his household prayers) for all wise, prudent and discreet apprentices and subordinates who do their masters' will, and have their masters' welfare ever and always at heart; and more solemnly than any other present did Billy Brogan respond to this.

When the prayers were ended, another fire was made, for sociability's sake only, and we squatted around it listening to stories. Toal and Pat and Billy drew upon their store of the old, old tales of our people; and the Master charmed us with an account of the wonderful siege of Troy, elevated us with the story of Socrates, and melted us with the pathetic narrative of Æneas. Finally, Ellen Burns led in a hymn, which, waking the deep stillness of midnight, sounded startlingly along the lake, and sent up from their beds three moor birds that circled overhead till the last stave died away, and then wandered off to seek security farther from the strange company. When the hymn was finished the softest knowe was chosen and given to Ellen and Nuala; Billy and I took to ourselves another choice knowe, and the Master, Toal, and Pat chose likewise as best they could; and all stretched their tired limbs to woo repose with the wavelets crooning the faintest fairy lullaby in our ears.

Brisk and fresh, we were afoot while yet the sun was very low and the shadows very long next morning; and being seen from the island by the pilgrims who, after a night's watching and praying, were coming out of prison, a boat soon put off for us and brought us to the island in good time to hear the first Mass of the day.

The island was so small that clear over it lengthwise I could cast a picked pebble. Yet on it there were several hundred penitents. Two chapels and several houses for lodging the pilgrims stood along the water's edge; the Station Beds were grouped in the rocky centre.

Very soon after Mass the making the Stations began. All the penitents went bare-headed and bare-footed; and the gravel and sharp stones tried the feet and knees of many severely. The whole surface of the little island was thickly dotted with devotees—some by St. Bridget's Cross, standing with arms extended and solemn faces looking upward in the act of renouncing with solemn voice the World, the Flesh and the Devil; some standing in the laving waters of the lake praying toward the East; many kneeling on the shingles by the water's edge supplicating God with intense speech; and some hundreds telling their beads as they walked and ran the rounds of the rocky beds or knelt on the pebbles amongst them—the atmosphere of the whole island filled with the great, stirring, thrilling, Heaven-ascending murmur of pleading prayer which ceases not ever, day or night, from June's first morning till August's Day of Our Lady. The scene and the sound certainly stirred and thrilled me to my soul's centre; and when I looked off at the great wild wastes of moor that stretched far and far on every side, and the girdle of frowning hills beyond, which seemed effectually to shut off from the world the Loch of the Holy Island, and then gazed upon the scene immediately around me, where every soul openly communed with a present God, I in my unsophisticated pure state of mind found the spiritual within me utterly and completely, for the time being, overmaster and annihilate the sensual. I trod on thin air through spirit-land, and I experienced the taste of that exultant joy which disembodied souls must know.

Though many walked the Stations singly, the penitents generally went in bands, led by a devout old man or woman, who, having done the pilgrimage often, was fitted to guide and direct the others through the multiplicity of prayers and intricacies of the Stations without hesitation or mistake.

Toal, by prerogative, led our little band. With beads in hand we began by visiting the altar of St. Patrick's chapel, from which we trooped to St. Patrick's Cross, without, and to St. Bridget's Cross, kneeling before each and offering a short prayer. In turn, each stood with back to this Cross, and arms out-stretched, and thrice cried aloud our renouncement of the World, the Flesh and the Devil; after which we made the circuit of St. Patrick's chapel seven times, responding to the decade which Toal led in every round. St. Bridget's Bed, St. Brendan's Bed, St. Catherine's and St. Colmcille's we next visited in turn, making the outside and inside circuits of each three times, kneeling at the entrance to each Bed, kneeling again at the Cross in the centre, and responding (always aloud) to three Paters-and-Aves, and chorussing the Creed for each circuit both without and within, and for each kneeling. And at the large Penitential Bed, which includes two smaller we doubled the several exercises. Next, Toal hobblingly led the way over the pebbles to the Loch, in the waters of which we stood, looking eastwards, while we chanted further prayers, and again repeated these, kneeling by the water's edge. A prayer at St. Patrick's Cross, and prayers in St. Patrick's Chapel, concluded the station.

We were now glad enough to rest us and ease our aching feet upon the one lonely green knowe in the little island. Here many others were resting, too. It was a delight to observe as I did, that within the Holy Island all social barriers were levelled. A titled lady conversed in sisterly intimacy with a ragged-coated poor fellow, who, though he had never in his life been beyond the rough mountains of Donegal, discoursed to her as freely and with as little sense of shyness as if he spoke to Bride in the windy cabin at home.

An American bishop, a white-haired old country woman in homespun skirt, and a wealthy Australian, made a trio in an interesting discussion upon the changing social conditions of Ireland. Toal bestowed the favour of his company and the weight of his long experience and keen observation upon this latter group, to the great satisfaction of the Bishop, who, as Toal proceeded to discourse in his own imposing manner, leant forward and listened with whetted interest to a man who evidently knew his subject and how to treat it. Billy and Pat took their seats behind Toal, and, in modest pride for Knockagar and him, hung upon Toal's every syllable. An elegant and gentlemanly young man, observing Ellen from a distance came forward, ascended the knowe, and respectfully addressing her seated himself beside her without ceremony, and engaged her in conversation. The Master, standing up, held an audience of old women spell-bound, whilst he discoursed learnedly, and with wealth of allusion, upon penances and punishments in the early and middle ages of the Church, as well as amongst non-Christian peoples. Nuala and I watched, and wondered at all.

After an hour Toal shook his beads at us and said, "Come childre," whereupon the six of us trotted after him to begin the second Station—a repetition of the first. And we began our third and last compulsory Station about an hour after the conclusion of the Second.

Yet, neither on this nor on the succeeding days did we confine ourselves to the prescribed exercises, but made many further Stations for our own private intentions. Pat in particular and Toal, must have made Stations for every neighbour in Knockagar, so constantly all the day long did they trot the trying gravelly rounds. Little Nuala, with her wee white, soft feet, was unable, though, to walk much more than what was absolutely requisite; accordingly, in consideration of her sitting upon the green knowe and joining me in prayer and spirit whilst I ran the rounds, I agreed to allocate to her half the benefit of all my extra Stations. The other half I bestowed principally upon my uncle Donal, and partly upon Ellen Burns. When Billy Brogan heard of my arrangement he ran three extra Stations specially for Nuala, or Nuala's intentions. And he imparted to me in secret that he was dividing the benefit of all his other extra Stations between Corney Higarty, for whom were three or four, and (whisperingly) Ellen Burns, for whom were all the remainder.

Though we had had, during the day, as much boiled and sweetened Loch water as we cared to drink, it was with ravenous appetites we at six o'clock in the evening sat down to our first and only meal; a meal, simple and satisfying, composed of unbuttered hard-baked oaten cake and uncreamed tea—the single meal allowed each pilgrim on each of the three days of pilgrimage.

Than after this repast, I have seldom felt, before or since, more heartily satisfied. After vespers and sermon, the pilgrims gathered upon the green knowe, engaging in pleasant converse, walked around the Island's edge, or rowed off to visit the other wild islets of the Loch, singing hymns upon the waters as they went. Nuala had already made many friends who came around her on the knowe, questioning and chatting to her, to Billy Brogan's delight. But I believe Billy's greatest pride, as well as Pat's, and indeed the pride of all of us, was to observe, as we now did, Toal-a-Gallagher all but arm in arm with the American Bishop who vouchsafed him uncommon deference and wrapt attention, as they paraded back and forth upon the green stretch by the boat quay, Toal all the while discoursing with the fluency and ease of manner of a man to whom Bishops were as common as peeled potatoes.

On that, our first night on the Island, we were to watch and pray. So, at ten o'clock we entered Prison in St. Patrick's Chapel. Here Toal, who considered himself the proper man to lead the few hundred prisoners in prayer through the night, generously offered to his friend the Bishop the distinguished privilege. And his Lordship, with becoming acknowledgment of the honour done him, drew forth his beads and stepped forward to the altar-rails to comply, when a red-haired rag-dressed beggarman who bore around his neck a rosary of immense beads, and who, I afterwards learnt, was known as The Pilgrim, gave both Toal, and the Bishop a withering look, strode between the latter and the altar-rails, knelt down, and in stentorian voice began the recital of the prayers, to which instantly the congregation thundered response.

The Bishop meekly bowed acquiescence, as to the prerogative of a better man, and, stepping aside, knelt behind a pillar, from which he joined devoutly in the prayers. In the tone of Toal's responses I was sorry to hear a defiant ring unusual in devotional exercises.

Yet, indeed, the Pilgrim proved himself a competent leader, except that he put too many and too original trimmings to his Rosaries. Amongst many other remarkable prayer requests, I well remember that he asked us to "Say one pather-anavvy for the holy priests of this diocese of Clogher, now in spiritual and mortual retreat in Inniskillen, that God may return them to their sorrowin' flocks safe by both sea and land, well in soul, and sound in wind and limb;" and *"Wan other pather-anavvy for the sufferin' poor souls in Purgatory, that the doores of that Institution may rot and dhrop from their hinges, and so give re-laisement to the fathers, mothers and brothers, kith, kindhred and kin, of everybody congregated here this holy night."

The Pilgrim grudgingly enough vouchsafed us

*I know well that these prayers will read like extravagant exaggerations, yet they are, substantially, prayers asked for by The Pilgrim.—(S. MacManus).

intervals of rest from prayer, during which hymns were sung, or holy conversation joined in. But he turned these pauses to good account by going through the chapel, staff in hand, and cracking on the head, or pummeling in the ribs, any poor, wearied individual, whom drowsiness was involuntarily getting the better of. Poor Billy Brogan earned one venomous knock, which left him rubbing his head for a good while after; and I fear that I smiled through my prayers so grievously that I felt constrained to make it a matter of confession after. The Pilgrim's staff was a fine tonic; for, any one who got a taste of it was enabled to fight sleep afresh for another hour, when the chances were that he got another dose; and thus were the over-weary ones helped along till morning.

On the night succeeding, notwithstanding awkwardly crowded quarters, we were heartily glad to let fall our heavy eyelids, and get one round and sound sleep, the first permissible in forty hours.

Yet did Toal have us afoot, and trotting the stations again, at an hour when still the shadows lay long across the Island. Despite the fatigue of the past three days, Nuala, I rejoiced to find, was fresh and bright and joyous, and ran the stations with new energy. Ellen, too, was radiant. And, indeed, the sun on all faces that morning seemed the outward manifestation of the sun that was certainly in every soul. At Mass, with at least two hundred other communicants we approached the altar, cleansed and purified as all now felt, and crowned our joy there.

Of the American Bishop—who accompanied him to the boat—Toal took a farewell that was almost affectionate, when we were about to embark. Thirty-five pilgrims, who crowded the boat, and weighed it nearly to the water-edge, bowed down to receive the Prior's parting benediction, and were then slowly rowed off from the Island—all of them sweetly sad at quitting the Island of Spiritual joy, and some of them (including Ellen and Nuala) softly weeping. All of us looked longingly and lovingly at the holy spot, at the pilgrims who stood on the shore waving their farewells, at the many, who, with bent heads and moving lips, were treading the mazes of the stations, at the sunny green knowe, the little houses, the Priory, the two Chapels, the Beds, the stones even with which we had grown so intimate, and we stood up in the boat and cried aloud our farewells to all—all, and waved caps and handkerchiefs.

"Sit down, now," said the boatman.

Then, as we sat, one of the oarsmen raised the "Farewell to Loch Dearg," which was always sung on such occasions, and was instantly joined therein by every voice in the boat. Come-all-ye though its air was, and poor its literary value, I, on that morning, thought it unsurpassed and unsurpassable as a heart-tribute to the Isle we were sorrowfully quitting; and as the big black boat, with its load, crawled over the shimmering waters of the Loch, getting gradually farther and farther away from the spot toward which all eyes were wistfully turned, the strains of the song joined in by nearly two score voices that quivered with emotion, certainly made it, to us then (and to many of us still), the grandest poem that ever was penned, and most beautiful song that ever was sung.

I hazard it here in all the coldness of bald print, and I only ask the critically disposed to remember that the words are hallowed by being sung, through long years, by many, many thousands of happy pilgrims who in purity of heart and exaltation of soul, are quitting the Isle where they found relief and consolation, and returning with all the renewed and aggressive energy which God's grace imparts, to fight the world once more.

As we wended our way home over the shining hills there was happiness in all hearts. The Master and Ellen went together. Nuala walked, by choice, by my side, whilst Billy Brogan took position on one side of her. I held Nuala's hand as we tramped the sunny heather, all three talking joyously of many things—though a sobriety which we two realised not tempered the joy of poor Billy.

Farewell to Loch Dearg.

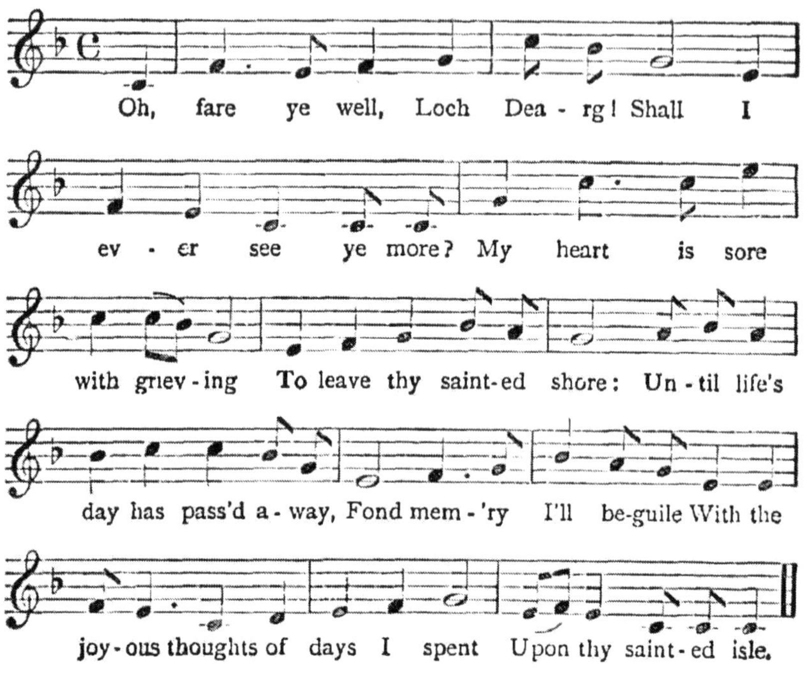
Oh, fare ye well, Loch Dea - rg! Shall I
ev - er see ye more? My heart is sore
with griev - ing To leave thy saint-ed shore: Un - til life's
day has pass'd a - way, Fond mem - 'ry I'll be-guile With the
joy - ous thoughts of days I spent Upon thy saint - ed isle.

Saint Patrick was its founder,
  At Heaven's express command,
To cleanse away the sinful stains
  Of his own loved Ireland;
In hopes by prayer and penance here
  God's mercy to secure,
Lest punishments hereafter
  For them we may endure.

He blessed with sweet devotion
  This penitential isle;
He chose as its director
  St. Dabheoc without guile;
While hosts of saints and hermits here
  True happiness did find,
By leaving home and worldly joys
  And kindred all behind.

Throughout each station season,
  From every distant clime,
The children of St. Patrick
  Frequent this Holy Shrine,
Each pilgrim here is edified
  With piety sincere,
And it's here each soul is purified
  By penances severe.

But when the Holy Island
  Is fading out of view,
With tears the grateful pilgrims
  To it they bid adieu,
Saying, "May its name still spread abroad,
  Its fame grow greater still,
Its Patron Saint still honour'd be,
  And crowds its cloisters fill."

So fare you well, Loch Dearg,
  Shall I ever see you more ?
My heart is filled with sorrow
  To leave thy sainted shore.
Until life's days shall pass away
  With pleasure shall I dwell
On the happy days I spent with you,
  Loch Dearg, fare thee well.

CHAPTER XXII.

THE FALL OF DUNBOY—AND OF THE VAGABONE.

THE Siege of Dunboy Castle on Bantry Bay, towards the close of Queen Elizabeth's reign, the final and most brilliant exploit in the rebellion of Hugh O'Neill, appealed to the imagination of all of us, but particularly to that of the Vagabone, who mightily admired MacGeoghagan, for that after a long and valiant, but vain, defence of the Castle, he had made a dying effort to reach, with a torch, the powder-store, and thus destroy in the ruins the English assailants, together with himself and his handful of brave comrades. Often, by special request, I read to the Vagabone and the boys the thrilling narrative; and often did the Vagabone express the wish to "reh'arse" it.

It was in the October which followed our pilgrimage, that, a grand opportunity presenting itself, the

Fall of Dunboy was re-enacted—with consequences unanticipated by most of us.

On a day on which Corney had fastened his cabin door, and gone to Donegal to draw his pension, the Vagabone sped his messengers North and South, and East and West, to bid his lieges hastily in.

"This day," he said to the assembled band, "we've got the grandest of opportunities for reh'arsin' the Siege and Fall of Dunboy. Corney's gone to dhraw his pension, and by right of the rules o' war we'll enter and take possession of his little house, and take care of it for him while he's gone—and we'll hold the Siege of Dunboy there. I'll be MacGeoghagan meself, and I'll only ax five picked men to garrison the Castle with me; all the rest of the crowd of ye 'ill be the attackin' English under Carew. We'll store plenty of arms and amminition, and we'll barricade the Castle—then yous may use every mains lawful in war to storm and to take the place. Don't spare yerselves, boys, for yous may never have such an opportunity again. And I promise ye we, the brave and gallant defenders, 'ill not spare ourselves."

Some one asked, "What about blowin' up the Castle, Toal?"

"That's provided for," young Toal replied, exhibiting two brown paper packets. "Me father, as good luck would have it, was intendin' to do a bit of blastin' in the quarry-fiel' for the new byre he's goin' to build. Matt McCourt fetched him a supply of blastin' powder from Donegal a-Sathurday last. Here's two packages of it—and a wee piece of fuse."

The completeness of the plan was vouchsafed a cheer from the boys. The Vagabone chose his five men; and the English forces were then drawn off to await the signal to begin.

The Vagabone, in the defensive, stayed the door, and for offensive purposes removed (forcibly) the two little windows—front and back—which the house contained. Just then he remembered that he should float a standard over Dunboy. He had not anything at hand quite appropriate, but he drew upon the utmost resources of the besieged garrison. Three fishing rods of Corney's, bound together, made indeed a strong and excellent flagstaff; but for the flag the exigencies of circumstance could afford him, unfortunately, nothing more fitting, or, I regret to say, more artistic, than a grey flannel article of wear belonging to Corney which the average man could never muster enough audacity to flaunt in the public eye. But as the Vagabone was no average man, or boy, he coolly fastened the article in question to a rodline, planted the rod upon the chimney—from inside—and then ran up his flag, which, when it was blown out full length by the breeze, looked more a forked pennant than a regular flag. Contrary to the usages of war the English cheered their enemy's standard lustily.

All preparation being now completed, the Vagabone gave the whistle-signal, and the siege, destined to be memorable in the annals of Knockagar began.

Of the little garrison, two were placed to defend and offend—particularly offend—at each window; one was told off to supply ammunition—which took the shape of stones of all sizes; and young Toal himself took possession of the chimney, out of which, popping up his head and shoulders, he hailed deadly volleys on the charging foe, suddenly withdrawing as return volleys whizzed where his head had been.

There was a deal of destruction, it is true, wrought amongst the enemy as they advanced; but it only made them quicken their charge, till, very soon, they were boldly attempting to swarm in by both windows and chimney; only to be ignominiously thrust back, however, every time, covered with many and grievous wounds, from oaken sticks and long poles. But, at an early stage in the fight, they forced the Vagabone's standard from the chimney top, and bore it off amid tumultuous rejoicing.

Repeated and valiant as were the dashes of the attacking force, the invincible six within seemed likely to hold the fort till the dread presence of the returned Corney would induce them to evacuate with a haste unbecoming brave soldiers, had not the enemy planned a new form of attack. Accordingly, whilst three detachments were told off to keep the defenders busy at windows and chimney, another three parties proceeded, one to force or break the door, whilst another opened a passage in the gable, and the third removed a portion of roof.

The plan was so effective that, in a short time the English came dropping and tumbling pell-mell through the roof, on the heads of an astonished garrison. Thick and fast they came tumbling down, and, engaging in a hand-to-hand fight with the defenders, were, from sheer force of numbers, overcoming the latter, when, suddenly, at the barricaded door there was a great burst of flame and smoke and a terrific report; defenders and attackers, from fright or from force, fell over in mingled heaps, and portions of the barricades rained on, and around, them.

"MacGeoghagan may die, but Dunboy and Ireland is avenged," they—or rather such of them as were enough collected—heard the Vagabone cry. And then he shot through a window. "Carry out now your dead and your wounded," he called in, "and let them that still lives come and answer the rowl-call."

It was only when the ardour of battle was departed that the dire mischief wrought upon Corney's little cabin, and the consequences likely to ensue, dawned forcefully upon all. The door was not any more; the portable articles which had been within were smashed; the windows were gone; the gable was broken in; the roof was laid open. Every one was in distress and sorrow.

"Corney himself 'ill be here inside two hours," said the Vagabone, light-heartedly. "Then there'll be music. The farther yous is off from it, boys, the better yous 'ill like it. I'm gone for Augherbeg, meself."

"How long do ye think ye'll stay away, Toal?" some already lonely one asked.

Toal, before replying, allowed his eye once more to range over all the wrecked cabin.

"The bether part of twelve months, I b'lieve," he then replied, gravely. "Good-bye, boys! Good-bye!"

Then he was gone, lightly skipping over ditches and hedges as he departed across country in a bee line for Augherbeg.

At many an erstwhile peaceable hearth in Knockagar there were loud and wrathful words that night; and many a tearful youth crawled to bed both sore and supperless. In Toal a-Gallagher's, words were higher and more painful than in any other home; they were exchanged chiefly between Susie Gallagher, who flamed indignant, and Corney Higarty, who bore himself indeed no worse, and no more insolently, than might be expected from a much-outraged man. Toal himself, who pegged and sewed viciously whilst raging storm filled his house, maintained a silence that was painful; and poor Billy Brogan a silence that was piteous.

Poetical justice was in a measure satisfied by Corney Higarty sleeping away a portion of his wrath in the Vagabone's bed, which, on that night and until his own hut was by kind neighbours' help made habitable again, he occupied under protest.

Next morning at an early hour Toal a-Gallagher, taking with him a good, stout and well-tested stick, set out for Augherbeg. He returned at night disappointed; for the Vagabone, warned of his coming, had unceremoniously quitted his uncle's. Toal said little, which was ominous. During the next ten days, in company with the same stout oaken staff, he paid not less than four surprise visits to Augherbeg—in vain. This looked so like determination on his father's part, that the poor Vagabone concluded he should look out for a more tolerant master and a more appreciative world.

Two weeks later, Pat the Pedlar, arriving from Ballyshanny, where he had been to purchase supplies, took out from amongst the archives which he preserved inside his hat crown, and presented to Toal a-Gallagher, a crumpled and much soiled letter. "This letter," he said, "was left in Misther Mulhern's, where I buy me goods, for me to fetch to you."

"Who's it from?" Toal asked, as, laying aside the boot upon which he wrought, he examined it round and over.

"I suppose it'll maybe tell that inside," Pat said.

Billy Brogan stayed the awl in its course through a tough sole; and Susie, leaving the floor half swept, came forward with heather besom in hand; and Pat, too, leant forward eagerly; whilst Toal opened the letter, turned it inside out, settled his spectacles, resettled them, and then announced in surprised tones, "Why, it's from that vagabone!"

"No?" said Susie in alarm.

Billy Brogan's eye brightened. "What does the poor divil say, Toal?" he asked eagerly.

"'Dear father and mother,'" Toal began, "'I take up my pen and ink to write you these few lines, hoping it will find you in the same state of health, thank God, it leaves me, and wants to say

I have hired on board the *Thrasher* as a cabin boy to go out to the States, and sails this evening with God's help, and wants to say I forgive both of yous for all old scores, and wants to say to Corney Higarty I forgive him, too, and goes away without no grudge against him or against anybody, and wants to say, too, that I'm going to settle down in the States when I reach them and make my fortune, and please God I'll send yous lots and leavings of money, and I'll send my mother the best dhress of all silk and satin that money can buy, and a blue cloak with a hood down to her heels——' "

A tear blabbed right down upon the very line Toal was reading. "Woman!" said he, stamping his foot and looking up to where Susie bent above him, "will ye houl' your tongue, I say."

Poor Susie had not spoken, and did not speak—perhaps could not.

Toal, after a moment's hesitation, during which he drew a long breath, resumed—

"'And a bonnet like Father Dan's flower-garden, and I'll send you a prayer-book and a castor hat, and Billy Brogan——' "

"God bliss 'im," Billy blurted.

"'A watch and a chain that'll go eight days like Matthew McCourt's clock——' "

"May the Lord bliss the ginerous poor fella," Billy said, in a voice that trembled.

"'And a castor hat like yours to Father Dan, and a history book of all the great wars of the world to Corney (who I forgive), and a parrot that can speak the seven languages to the Widow's Pat, and another castor hat and a book of the most wonderful prophecies to be had for money to John Burns, and presents of all kinds to every one else, tell them all, and when I come back, a gentleman, with a goold watch and chain and a nice black suit and grand talk, like Pathrick Brogan of Ardban, they'll be music at Knockagar, I tell you, and isn't it yous 'll be glad and proud to see me then, and ask everybody to pray for me, and I'm praying for everybody, and I forgive and forget everything and everybody with all my heart and soul, and tell them that, and tell Corney, and God bliss yous all, and now I must lay down my pen and finish your affecting son, Toal. P.S.—And don't forget to tell Corney I forgive and forget him and everybody, and I'll write soon and send yous plenty of money when I land.'"

Susie went down to the room, and closed out the door. Toal again took up the shoe upon which he had been working. Billy Brogan likewise resumed his work.

Pat the Pedlar afterwards told how he sat for a long time neither speaking nor spoken to—sat, too, motionless, for he felt a sense of guilty shame if even his chair creaked. When, at length, the long-continued silence had grown too painful for him, he raised his pack slowly and quietly, and with a nod of his head to Toal and Billy, neither of whom observed it, slid out of the house.

And Knockagar was destined to know the poor Vagabone's presence no more for long years.

CHAPTER XXIII.

BONFIRE NIGHT.

WHEN the shades of late, late, evening came slowly sifting down on midsummer night, the boys began gathering from the glens and the dales, wending their way in twos and threes and half-dozens to the top of Knockdiara hill, every one bringing with him as much as he could drag of whins, *brasna*, limbs of trees, bogfir, turf, or broken boxes. And after these toiling groups came bands of merry girls, some shawled, some unshawled, who made the evening ring with merry laughter. And, finally, the old men and wiseheads of the countryside, followed, stepping soberly and chatting gravely, reaching the crown of the hill when the immense heap of firing had been piled by the youngsters and lighted.

And just when our bonfire was lighted, we could see, as our eyes for the purpose searched the dark landscape, little flames begin to flicker at various points, anear and afar; for, this was the night of summer nights to which all people—the youngsters for the honour and glory, and the old ones for the luck and grace, of their own district—looked forward with joyous anticipation, and on which every one felt bound to exert himself to make the bonfire of his own townland out-rival not alone that of his neighbours', but all the scores of hill-top fires which would be seen radiating away and away to the far horizon—that horizon itself being on this night traceable by the ring of fiery diamonds which studded it.

We rejoiced to find that we were amongst the first to light up in all the landscape. We watched and named the other fires, as, one by one, from time to time they leapt up after ours. "There goes the Dhrimadiara one, boys!" "And the Dhrimore Hill one!" "No, that's Tullylagan!" "See, the Dhrimholm hills goin' up, lads!" "Do ye mind the blaze they have in Rossnowlagh!" "Ay, see it in the wathers!" "Thonder (yonder) goes Augherbeg!" "Phew! it's out again on them!" "They have it lit again!" "It's out again!" "No, it's people passin' atween the flame and us'—Don't ye see how it's blazin' now!" "A poor show, thon they have on Altcor the night!" "Ay, they're payin' someone to houl' a rush-light!"

"Now, Killymard goes up!" "Now Killymard goes out!" "Now it goes up again—a brave blaze, in faith!" "Ach, see how thick they've got on the other side of the wather!" "A beautiful blaze, boys, on Kildoney Point!" "Beautiful! See it in the say!" "What's wrong with Doorin, the night?" "They're scarce of kindlin'!" "Or someone spit on the makin's!" "Look at Dhrimconnor!" "See Glencoagh, too!" "Did any of yous ever see as poor a blaze on Killian?" "Or on Meenagran?" "How thick they've got all over, lads!" "I didn't see a better showin' these five years!" "They're like stars on a frosty night, if ye'd paint the sky black!" "They're thicker nor stars!" "Och, there's few fires as fine as our own!" "There's no fire of them all as fine as ours!" "Knockagar always took the lead!" "And always houl's it!" "Three hearty cheers, boys, for the best bonfire within the sky—our own!"

And three ringing cheers were given; an answer to which we could just faintly hear coming from some of our nearest rivals.

Our great high-piled fire was now leaping far in flame-tongues, flinging and waving its yellow sheet of light down the hill, and across the valley, and flaunting it over Knockagar itself. A host of children were bounding and clapping their hands, around it. The boys and girls made matters lively with merry badinage; and older heads looked on in smiling approval.

Billy Brogan, of course, was soon asked for a song, and "Billy Brogan's song!" was, thereupon, vociferously clamoured for by all.

Billy, modestly, wanted to sing from the outskirts of the gathering, but he was forcibly led within the circle, and placed in full light of the bonfire, where, all shyly and blushingly, he announced that he would give them "Bold Brennan on the Moor," a popular old ballad. And he sang, beginning in a low, nervous, but musical voice that charmed them, gradually raising his tones as courage came to him:—

It's of a fearless highwayman a story I will tell,
His name was Willie Brennan, in Ireland he did dwell,
And on the Livart mountains he commenced his bould career,
Where many a wealthy gentleman before him shook with fear.

Brave and undaunted stood bold Brennan on the moor!

A brace of loaded pistols he carried night and day,
He never robbed a poor man upon the king's highway,
But when he'd taken from the rich, he gave to them had less,
And always did divide with the widow in distress.

One day upon the highway, as Willie he sat down,
He met the Mayor of Cashel a mile outside the town;
The Mayor he knew his features; "I think, young man," said he,
"Your name is Willie Brennan—you must come along with me."

As Brennan's wife had gone to town, provisions for to buy,
When she saw her Willie taken she began to weep and cry;
He says, "Give me that tenpence!" As soon as Willie spoke
She handed him the blunderbuss from underneath her cloak.

Then with his loaded blunderbuss, the truth I will unfold,
He made the Mayor to tremble, and robbed him of his gold;
One hundred pounds was offered for his apprehension there,
He with his horse and saddle to the mountains did repair.

Then Brennan, being an outlaw upon the mountains high,
Where cavalry and infantry to take him they did try;
He laughed at them with scorn, until at length, 'tis said,
By a false-hearted young man he was basely betrayed.

In the county Tipperary, in a place they call Clonmore,
Willie Brennan and his comrade they did suffer sore;
He lay among the fern, which was thick upon the field,
And nine wounds he did receive before that he would yield.

Then Brennan and his companion, knowing they were betrayed,
He with the mounted cavalry a noble battle made;
He lost his foremost finger, which was shot off by a ball;
And Brennan and his comrade they were taken after all.

So they were taken prisoners, in irons they were bound,
And conveyed to Clonmel jail, strong walls did them surround;
They were tried and found guilty, the judge made this reply,
"For robbing on the King's highway, you are both condemned to die!"

"Farewell unto my darling wife, and to my children three,
Likewise my aged father—he may shed tears for me;
And to my loving mother, who tore her gray locks and cried,
Saying, 'I wish, Willie Brennan, in your cradle you had died!'"

When Billy had concluded, the Master—who always lent the honour of his presence to such gatherings—for the benefit of all, pronounced his opinion that "the exquisite melodiousness of William Brogan's vocal powers were yet unimpaired"—a pronouncement which, while it made Billy blush and retire, was warmly endorsed by the gathering. Many another country boy sang, and Nuala even, chaperoned by Corney Higarty and the Master, was forced to the front, smiling confusedly, and obliged "to contribute to the harmony of the nocturnal festivities," as the Master phrased it, and so charmingly and sweetly she did it that I was elated with pride for her, and I wanted to go forward and stand by her side also, and take to myself some of the honour which, as her sponsors, the Master and Corney were ostentatiously appropriating. "Though he's there himself to hear it," Corney announced, "I say that Billy Brogan, fine singer as he is, and very fine—I say that Billy, singin' beside little Nuala, is no more nor a yalla-yandherin beside a lark." And, though the eulogy of the universal favourite pleased every one there, it pleased none better than it did Billy.

"Corney's right," Billy said to those near him. "In troth, he's right. Only—he should 'a' sayed a crow beside a lark."

It was now the depth of midnight. All the dark

landscape, east and west and north and south, was starred with fires, some of which held their light aloft steadily, and many of which, like candles snuffed out and lighted again, were constantly appearing and disappearing as the people around those flames eclipsed them by moving into our line of vision. The sound of distant cheering or laughter, from those who made merry on other hills, was borne to our ears, during the rare lulls that occurred in the noisy merriment around our own fire, heightening our enjoyment by the knowledge that all the world was this night enjoying itself.

Again and again we had renewed our fire, piling it high each time, and cheering loudly, as every additional armful of fuel was flung into the great yellow maw that received it with roars of fierce delight.

We all listened with keen attention when the Master delivered to us a delectable discourse upon the fire-worship and fire-worshippers of the East, giving it as his opinion that our Milesian forefathers, when they came to Ireland long years ago, brought with them Sun-worship at least; and that this, Midsummer Night, was one of their chief festivals. He told us how Saint Patrick instead of attempting to eradicate the too firmly established Pagan customs, had diplomatically turned them into Christian observances. The holy wells that now restored to us spiritual and physical health, and the sacred fires that blessed our cattle, and our crops, and all our possessions, were instances. As weak humanity, he said, ever needs emblems—something it can see and touch—to stimulate the spiritual within it, these were some of the emblems which Patrick gave to his children to turn their minds to God and prayer. He expressed, in very grand language, the pleasure it gave him to find that notwithstanding the advance of what was named civilization—a civilization that very often, like the Juggernaut car, only pressed the souls out of those over whom it advanced—the old customs, and the old faiths, and the old ideals, were not yielding a jot in Knockagar. "Look around ye," said the Master, dramatically waving his arm over the countryside, "and enumerate, if you can, the conflagrations that, this night, aspire towards heaven from every noted eminence in all the land—each one of which is a tongue of hope speaking far and high the soulfulness of our country; on next Midsummer night enumerate the conflagrations once more, and, William Brogan"—for the rapt attention of Billy fascinated the Master—"if your reckoning is then one less (which may Providence forbid), conclude that there is one hope quenched for spiritual Ireland, one noble aspiration repressed, one ideal lost." To each suggested conclusion Billy solemnly bent his head. " But as I said," quoth the Master, " may Providence forbid! And in Him we have trust."

" We have," Billy said, sincerely; " we have." And many muttered, " we have."

" True words for the Masther, every wan of them," John Burns said. " And it's that same civilization he talks of that's dhrivin' away the fairies——"

" And dhrivin' away Luck with them," interposed Billy Brogan.

" And dhrivin' away Luck with them," said John, " Luck and Grace——"

" Luck and Grace," Billy echoed. " Ay, ay," and he shook his head.

" But in Knockagar, thank God," John went on, "and for far round it, the Gentry* are respected, and they in their turn befriend us. And the oul' customs are as well observed the day as I ever remimber them to be obsarved in my day."

" Yis," said Toal; " yis. And that's as it shud be."

" Our bonfire this night, too, is as fine and large and grand, and our gatherin' is as big and as merry, as, I might say, I've iver seen it."

But good as the bonfire was, and gay as was the gathering, all of the young people knew there was a want, and knew—though they scarcely cared to admit it—that the bonfire of this year was not

* The Fairies.

what it had been on preceding occasions. Billy Brogan, though, had the courage of his convictions. He spoke out more boldly than was usual with him before much company, saying:

"Beggin' your pardon, Misther Burns, for my imperence, but the bonfire this night is by no means what it was these other last years. And that, too, for very good raison," sorrowfully. "The life and the sowl of a bonfire, and the wan that made our bonfires what they were, he's not here this night; but whoiver sees him, whereiver he is this night, he's thinkin', thinkin' of the bonfire above Knockagar. God be with you, young Toal!" For a minute Billy seemed not to be one bit ashamed of the tears that came and looked out of his eyes; but, soon recollecting himself, he rubbed the back of his hand over his eyes and withdrew. When I looked to see how Toal the father took the reference, I found that he had retired also.

It was with especial regret we young people admitted to ourselves that the absence of the Vagabone had materially affected the usually marked superiority of the Knockdiara blaze over every other blaze on the countryside. For weeks before a bonfire night he was always busily engaged with his band, laying in stores of the best burning material to be had in the country. Billy knew, just as every staid man there knew, that the means employed by the Vagabone in collecting his material were better not inquired into with too scrupulous diligence. They knew well that the Vagabone chiefly gathered his stores by night, and that the darker the nights preceding a bonfire the greater and more glorious was apt to be the conflagration—and they knew well that many a poor man, attending previous fires, had unwittingly warmed himself by the blaze of his own byre door or been delighted with the glow of his own violated turf-stack—all this they every one knew, yet loftily forebore to recall.

"Though I say it that maybe isn't expected to say it," said Corney Higarty generously, "he was a warrior and a brave fella, and hadn't a bad bone in his body. If he had wracked meself instead of me worthless wee bit of a house, I couldn't say worse of him and stick to the truth."

"And an honest fella he was, says I," quoth Owen a-Slaivin', who evidently felt that it was only Christian-like for him, too, to publicly certify to the good character of the absent one. But when Owen talked of honesty I thought of my snares that still mysteriously parted with their captives ere my hand released these—and I shook my head. Yet when, later, I saw Billy thanking Owen with sincerity for the kindness of his testimony, I thanked him in my heart, too.

When after midnight, the last of our fuel had

been piled on, and was nearly burnt out, the fire was scattered, and our cattle driven through it, each one, as he or she drove, praying for a blessing on them and their produce for the next twelve months.

And then all took with them burning brands with which in hand they made the circuit of all their crops and of all their fields. The patch of the Widow's Pat was small indeed, but I ran with Nuala the circuit of the whole, and the circuits of his little bit of corn and his piece of potatoes, I leading in the Paters and Aves, and Nuala responding. In turn, then, Nuala came with me, and ran the circuits of Uncle Donal's crops, praying around them as fervently as she did around Uncle Pat's.

The hush of the depth of night was over the earth, but was broken often by sound of distant cries as from field to field neighbour called to neighbour, or a dog barked on a far-off hill.

Ten thousand stars were blinking down through the darkness; and we saw a hundred lights flitting through the fields, and knew that thereunder were a hundred pairs of hurrying feet encircling the crops, and a hundred low voices speaking to God, and a hundred hearts appealing to Him to save their all from ban and blight, and out of His bounty to bless with plenty the hastening harvest. Nuala and I, when we had finished our circuits and our prayers, stood for a long time, looking and listening, and speaking no word. The magic of the hour heightened the fascination of the scene, and our imaginations were filled to the point of enforced silence.

At length I thought, "All that I see and hear and feel now, is very like this life of mine looked at with half-closed eyes—this and my life are each a sort of dream. I wonder shall I ever awaken? and when? and how shall I feel when I do awaken? Will this blissful peace that has been mine as long as I remember, and the calm delight pass away from me? And will Knockagar pass away from me? And my uncle Donal, and Pat, and Billy, and Nuala, and all the lovable and loved people who are now a part of my life—or a part of my dream?"

There was a gulp in my throat at this. I stayed the race of my imagination till I dwelt long upon this.

"Do you know what I'm thinkin', Nuala?" I at length asked.

"No, Dinny, I do not," Nuala said.

"Come, let us move down the hill," I said, "till I lay ye at your own lane. Your uncle 'll be waitin' on ye."

I took Nuala's hand, and as we went down the fields I told Nuala of my strange thoughts.

"Well, Dinny," she said, with some surprise, when she had heard me out, "that's you always.

Always dhreamin'. And always thinkin' the most curious things that ever come into anybody's head —That ever come into nobody's head," she added emphatically.

"Well, the thoughts come, Nuala, and I must think them."

"I know that, Dinny," she said leniently.

"But, Nuala, do you never be thinkin' like that, about Knockagar? and your own pleasant life here? and your uncle Pat, and everybody?

"Indeed, I do not," she said. "I'll always have Knockagar, and Uncle Pat, and everybody—always"! she added with confident enthusiasm. "And it's a shame for you Dinny, that you do be thinkin' otherwise," she said.

We had got out on the high road, and had advanced on it as far as the end of Nuala's lane. Both of us sat down upon the ditch by the lane end.

After a little space of silent reflection I spoke again. I said:

"Ah, well, you're different, Nuala, anyhow. You can be with Knockagar and everybody, always. But I can't. I can't, Nuala," I said shaking my head.

"Oh, Dinny," she said with deep reproach, "have sense with ye."

"But I have sense, that's why I say it. See how big and how old I'm gettin', Nuala. In another year or two I must face and fight the world. Then I'll waken, Nuala, and the Lord knows where it is I'll find myself."

She said, in a tremulous voice, "Dinny, ye'll make me cry. Don't tell me that; for I couldn't bear to even think of ye ever leavin' Knockagar."

"Nuala," I said, "I wish't to God that I might'nt—I wish it to God."

"I wish it to God," said Nuala with fervour. "And I'll now always pray to God that you mayn't."

"God bless you, Nuala," I said, and I pressed my hands upon her yellow head. I knew that she let a teardrop fall as I did so, and my heart went out to my fond comrade with a deeper tenderness than I had before known for her.

"I would be sorry and sorry to part from you, Yellow Head," I said, "for I like you more than I can say. And I know that you like me."

"I like you, and I always liked you, very, very, very much—I always liked you more than anybody except my uncle Pat," she said calmly and unhesitatingly.

"I wisht I could thank you as much as I feel," I said.

"Why should you thank me," she said, lifting up serious eyes to me, "for doin' what I couldn't help doin'?"

I was silent for a minute. Then I said:

"When I was more of a child, Nuala, I used to like Ellen Burns, I thought, better than anybody else in the world."

"Yes, Dinny," Nuala replied, "and it used to make me more than half sorry, though I loved Ellen myself."

"But even then it would have been hard for me to lose as close and dear a comrade as what you were to me. And now—now—" I paused, and then shook my head.

"Then, Dinny," said Nuala rising, "sure you'll not be dhreamin' ill dhreams any more?"

"I'll try hard, Nuala," I said.

"And good-night, Dinny," Nuala said.

I took both of Nuala's hands between mine and pressed them there as I said, "Good night, Nuala: and God's blessin' go with ye always."

Nuala bent her head to the fervent prayer. Then she gently withdrew her hands from mine, and, turning, walked up the lane toward where the light was streaming from the little pane.

I turned and wended my way up our hill toward where a little light beaconed me, too. I was happy with a kind of sad happiness. At my uncle's door I turned and looked at the last few fires that, lingering on distant hills, still glimmered through the night, and hearkened to the few dying sounds that still floated over the silence rather than broke it, and then gazed down where, under a dark cloak, lay Knockagar: my gaze rested there for a while; then I raised my cap and I said, "May God keep ye always with me, Knockagar!" My eye took in the light, which was yet shining, in the window of the Widow's Pat. Then I lifted the latch of our door and went in.

CHAPTER XXIV.

AT UNCLE DONAL'S FIRESIDE AGAIN.

For twelve months and more I did try hard to dream no more ill dreams. And I was more than fairly successful. I roamed the scrugs, and the glens, and the woods, as if I were still a child: and I fished, and I snared, and I dreamt the pleasant dreams of old; and I sat by Pat's fireside, or by Corney's, or Toal's, or John Burns's at night, listening as eagerly as ever to the always interesting, and ofttimes exciting, debates that were nightly waged around one hearth or the other. On my Sunday rambles Nuala was my most constant companion, and ofttimes we had the benefit, too, of Billy Brogan's entertaining company.

On a Sunday night in late October, Nuala, Billy, and I, had had a happy moonlight ramble on the hills, talking buoyantly (I well remember) of Ireland's hopes; for even Billy, who was inclined to be pessimistic, had been infused with the hopeful spirits of myself and Nuala, and had consented to see and acknowledge for our poor country a future in the near distance haloed with a radiant halo; and, on a hill-top he had sung for us, with inspiriting ring, that lovely Irish hymn of hope for our country, and encouragement in her affliction, *An Roisín Dubh*, or The Little Black Rose—one of the many figures by which the spirit of Éire was typified by the old Gaelic bards who sung of her when such an act was treason.

When, after parting with Billy at Toal's, and with Nuala at her own lane-end, I meandered up our own hill, and, lifting the latch, entered our door, I found my uncle Donal sitting in the corner, smoking.

"Dinny, had you a pleasant night out?" he asked me.

"I had a happy night, Uncle Donal," I said. And I detailed for him an account of our evening. "It was a very happy night," I said. "And," I added—for I knew such intelligence rejoiced his fond heart—"it's many's the happy night and happy day I do have, Uncle Donal."

My uncle Donal bestowed on me a look in which was a world of tender kindness. He did not speak then; but after a few moments turned his gaze into the fire, and fixed it there.

After a good while he raised his eyes to my face again, and he said:

"Dinny, boy, do ye know what night is this?"

I reflected for a little, and then shook my head.

"No, Uncle," I said, "I don't know."

"This is the twenty-seventh of October; and on this night, eighteen years ago, you were born."

I bowed my head to this. It was only then I recollected that this was my birth-night.

"While you were off, the night, Dinny, I've been sittin' here thinkin'—thinkin' a great deal—about you."

"Yes, Uncle?" I said, with some concern; for in my uncle's tone there was more than usual sadness.

"Your poor father and mother—may God rest their souls!" he began.

"May God rest them!" I repeated, in a low voice.

"I promised them," said he, "to be a father to ye, and to do everything that lay in me power for ye."

"And from Heaven's floor, Uncle Donal," I said, "they see how well you've kept yer promise."

"I wish it. I wish it," he said with a sigh.

"But I know it," I said, with fervour.

"I dhreamt of doin' great things for ye, Dinny, at one time, and givin' ye a great chance," he said.

"Ye got me on your back, Uncle Donal, and carried me to school—I mind it well—when I wasn't able to walk it, and on days when ye thought it too cold for me to walk it. And ye put the bone through the skin since, workin' two men's work, so that I might never miss a day at school," I said.

"Dinny," said he, "that's nothin'. There was once, and I thought with God's help I could put ye farther." He paused for a minute. "Ye're now eighteen years of age, a young man, gone as far as the Masther can put ye, and the cleverest boy (as he always boasts) that he has ever passed through his hands: and—and—Dinny—I can't do anything more for ye."

The painful effort which the last sentence cost him smote me to the heart.

"Uncle Donal," I said in pathetic appeal, "what more could you do for me?"

He simply shook his head, slowly, from side to side.

"This isn't just the sort of talk for your birth-night, Dinny," he said, after a little. "But you're a man any more, and I feel I must speak to ye like a man. Believe me, Dinny, I sthruggled hard with meself, afore ye come in, the night, wanting for not to talk to ye on this subject—but I found I had to—that I was bound to."

He paused again, gazing into the fir-flame. I looked into the flame, too, thinking deeply.

"It always seemed my lot, Dinny, to have to sthruggle hard with the worl'. And the worl' seemed always, by little and little, getting the better of me. But for the past ten years, and more especially for the past five, it was a one-sided sthruggle entirely."

I drew my stool close over by my uncle Donal, and I laid my hands, one over the other, on his knee. He put a big hand on top of them, and gave them a gentle pressure.

"Dinny," he said, "'tis sore enough sthrugglin' even-hands with the worl'; but when the worl' gets the upper hand, and keeps it, then it is that the heart of one gets sick."

I said, "Uncle Donal, what is the reason ye've kept me in the dark about this?" I spoke in piteous tones. I felt my own heart sicken, as my knowledge of my uncle's sad secret burst upon me.

"What use, Dinny?" he only said. "What use?"

"And I so happy all these years," I said, gazing into the fire with misty vision, "and you so miserable!"

"Miserable? No!" my uncle said with vigorous voice. "I was happy always to see you, Dinny, me brave boy, so happy. It was the knowledge of your happiness, under God, that bore me up."

"Ah! Uncle Donal, you shouldn't have let me go on being as idle-hearted and as thoughtless, as what —I now see—only now—I was. A thoughtless, thoughtless fellow! Ah! Uncle Donal.

"Dinny!" he said appealingly, "sure ye wouldn't add to my throuble?"

I bent my head till my forehead rested on the back of his hand where it lay upon my hands; and in another instant a flood of tears came.

My uncle placed his other hand upon my head, and I felt it tremble as, in silence, he held it there.

After a while, when my rush of tears was stayed, he said in a low voice, "Dinny boy, you were never thoughtless, you. Ye couldn't know what I chose to hide well from ye. Ye couldn't help, Dinny; and why, why then, should I try to rob ye of yer innocent enjoyment? And as I held it from ye for your own good before, 'tis for your own good now that I tell it to ye the night. Ye're a man now, and ye must know what ye have to face."

The words "Ye're a man now" aroused the drooping spirit within me, suddenly, and it braced itself. I lifted up my head, and sat erect, and looked my uncle in the eye. I said, in a calm voice that fell strangely on my own ear:

"Uncle Donal, tell me what's the worst?"

My uncle looked at me for a moment hesitatingly; but the next moment replied calmly,

"In five days more, Dinny—Hallowday—I'll be three years behind with the rent. I'm—not able to pay it. I'm threatened that it'll be let run no longer. I was born within these walls, Dinny"—his voice was tremulous here—"I've passed me life in them. I'm an old man now, and—and—" he paused whilst he braced himself with a long breath—"and, Dinny, it'll go hard on me to laive them for ever and see you laive them."

I did not relax one muscle in my countenance which was firm set. And I was all the more determined because I knew that Uncle Donal was with side glance narrowly observing me. Yet I never can tell the effort it cost me, for those words cut through and through the heart within me.

When I mustered enough nerve to speak without betraying all I felt, I said:

"Uncle Donal!" I was looking into the fire again.

"Well, Dinny boy?"

"I'm a man, now."

My uncle nodded his head. Then he said, rather soliloquizingly, "Ay, with a child's heart."

"A man," I repeated, with more firmness of voice, "and sthrong and able—thank God! In less than three weeks' time will be the Hirin' market in Donegal. I'll ask your blissin', Uncle, and God's, and I'll tie a few articles in a handkerchief, and go with the boys to the hirin' market. I'll hire meself to the Pettigo man that gives me most. I'll work for ye, Uncle Donal. Get sparin's for the rent and, with God's help, I'll pay it yet. Ye'll never bid good-bye to these walls, Uncle, while I can help it."

My uncle Donal's eyes grew moist as I spoke. "Dinny," he said when I had triumphantly finished, "Dinny—" and he placed a hand upon my head—"God 'ill bliss and prosper you yet. But—" his tone took on a stern firmness—"your father and mother's son 'ill never hire to a Pettigo man—'ill never stand up to be priced in a Hirin' market within the bounds of Irelan'."

"Uncle Donal!" I remonstrated, "sure it isn't any disgrace to ask honest money for honest work—in Ireland more than anywhere else?"

Yet his eyes flashed with the fire of a pride that I could not then, and can not now, rightly understand. He said, "One of your father's or mother's people never stepped on the stones of a Hirin' market; and, Dinny, while I live to prevent it you'll not be the first to do it. No!"

I felt confounded. I dropped my gaze, and reflected. After a minute my uncle laid a gentle touch on my shoulder and said, in tender tones,

"Forgive me, Dinny. Forgive me. But ye'll not do it, Dinny—ye can't do it."

After a while's thought I said,

"Then, Uncle, there's one other thing for me."

He looked into my eyes for a few moments, and then slightly inclined his head. "I suppose so," he said reluctantly.

"America," I said, with a voice that almost failed me.

"America," he repeated. "Yes."

But when it was said he buried his face in his hands, and broke down utterly.

CHAPTER XXV.

SYMPATHIZERS.

On the very next morning Uncle Donal and I set off early for Donegal, where, after inquiries regarding the ships that would be likely soon to sail for the States, we settled that I should go by *An Cailín Donn*, a little schooner of one hundred and twenty tons, which would weigh anchor from the Green Islands in the second week of November.

On that night I went over to John Burns's, bringing with me the making of a suit which my uncle had bought for me in Donegal. There were many of the neighbours assembled there.

"Didn't I make a shoot for ye last Aisther?" John asked half in surprise, and half in reproach. "And sure ye don't main ye're goin' to get another made?"

I said without raising my eyes to his face, "John, I am going away to America."

There was instantly a dead stop in the conversation that had been going on in the house. John pulled off his spectacles and looked at me in wonderment. He then said:

"What did ye say, chile?"

"I am going off to America on the *Cailín Donn* in a couple of weeks. It's time I was doing something to help my uncle Donal. And there's nothing to be had in Ireland."

All present had turned on their seats, and were observing me intently—except Nuala. I noticed that she did not turn towards me, or move. Ellen Burns got off the bench where she was sewing, and came and stood beside me, and put an arm round my neck.

"Dinny," said she, "surely, it's only a joke of ye."

I lifted up my eyes till they met Ellen's tender glance, and I said:

"It's too true, Ellen."

She took away her arm then, and went back and sat upon the table.

"To Amiriky?" said John, who had his eyes all the time bent upon me. To Amiriky!" He shook his head sadly. "And with your grand education, too, ye must go the road of all our poor boys—to Amiriky! Oh, *Mhuire, a's truagh!*"

"To Ameriky?" said the Widow's Pat. "To Amiriky! Och, och, for you, Dinny!"

"Yes," said Toal a-Gallagher, "To Amiriky! To Amiriky! Them's the words that's on the lips of all our Irish boys and girls now; and them's the words their broken-hearted mothers and fathers, croon and *caoine* to themselves, with shaking grey heads."

"And do ye blame the poor boys and girls, Toal?" asked Pat, in half reproach.

"No!" said Toal, "I don't blame them. I can't blame them. It's God knows that I don't, and can't."

"Who ever seen them goin' off, and witnessed them scenes that tear the hardest hearts—and could then think of blamin' them?" said John Burns.

I was still standing in the same spot, with bowed head, listening.

"But Dinny," said Billy Brogan, seeming only now to get his tongue loosed, "surely, surely, ye don't railly main to say that ye're goin' away from Knockagar, and from Irelan'—to laive everything and everybody?"

"I'm goin' away, Billy!"

"Goin' away! Goin' away!—Dinny!" he then said sternly. "What will your Uncle Donal do? What will Knockagar do? What will everybody do?

What," and here his tone melted into pathetic appeal, " what will Yalla Head do here—and meself? What, Dinny? And ye don't main to say that we'll never any more ramble the woods and the scrugs together?"

I went out of the house—almost with a stagger, and started homewards. But I had not gone a dozen yards till I found myself compelled to halt and lean upon the wall by the roadside, my head sunk upon my arm.

In another minute I found the hand that hung by my side taken hold of and clasped by two little hands that, without looking, I knew to be Nuala's.

" Dinny!" Nuala's voice whispered after a little. "Oh, Dinny! my heart's breakin' for ye! Is there nothin' for it but America? And to leave Knockagar? and to leave us all? Is there nothin', nothin', Dinny?"

I did not speak—could not speak—for a little. When I found my voice, I said, without yet looking upon her, " Nuala, there's nothin'."

She gathered my hand to her bosom, and clasped it there; and then warm tears rained on it—tears the touch of which instantly unlocked the dead weight of sorrow that lay upon my own heart; and my eyes streamed. And impulsively I clasped Nuala in my arms and pressed my lips upon hers. I still held her whilst I laid my lips on her white forehead, and softly on each deep eyelid, which drooped and closed to my kiss.

When I released her, I took both her hands—and they were trembling—between my own, and pressed them, though she was drawing from me.

"Nuala," I said, "Yellow Head, forgive me! Forgive me! but I couldn't but do it."

She laid a hand gently, very gently on my arm, said, "Dinny, poor boy, ye are forgiven. Good night!" Then she was gone.

CHAPTER XXVI.

FATHER DAN'S PRESENT.

My provision barrel, with its hinged lid lying open, stood in the kitchen a week before sailing day, and as our friends and neighbours from near and far dropped in from day to day with their presents of salted eggs, and potatoes, and bacon, and oaten cakes that had been hardening for many days, these presents were stowed away in the barrel. Though the *Cailín Donn's* average time in crossing the Atlantic was only nine weeks, still against emergencies that were not rare, I needed to take with me provisions for double that time.* Yet, ere the barrel had stood three days upon the floor, it overflowed; and though I did not need, and could

* The little passenger schooners that sailed out of Donegal Bay in those days were often three months, and sometimes more than four months, reaching New York.

not take, any further provisions with me, the presents still continued to arrive; so to avoid giving offence I was forced to practise a little pardonable deceit, and, hiding the barrel, accept all that was presented to me, when, going to the room under pretence of putting the donations in the barrel, I piled them on the table and on the chairs and on the floor.

All these little marks of neighbourly kindness, though the same would be extended to any poor boy or girl going from their midst, touched me deeply, and did not lighten the load of sorrow that weighted my breast at thought of leaving Knockagar and its loved and kindly ones, and going away into the strange world, where, amid throngs, every soul stood alone and lonely.

The coming of each sympathizing neighbour, and the presenting of each little token, deepened Uncle Donal's sorrow, too.

On an evening when I returned from the farther end of the parish, where I had, as in duty bound, been bidding farewell at every house, my uncle told me to go on down to Father Dan's, as he had had a messenger here for me.

Father Dan shook me by the hand with even more than his usual kindliness, when Kitty, the housekeeper, had led me into his room. The Master, who was seated there, likewise greeted me warmly. "Dionysius," he said, "it delights my soul to see thee."

"Sit ye down on that sofa there, Dinny, my boy," Father Dan said, "till we have a *seanach.* So you want to go the road they all go, do you, Dinny?" he said in a pathetic tone. "The road they all go! All!"

The pity in his voice was blended, I thought, with mild reproach.

"I don't want to go, Father Dan, God He sees," I said with a gulp in throat.

But Father Dan seemed not to notice my reply, for he had a far-away look in his eyes, and was shaking his head as if ruminating over his own sad thoughts.

"The road they all go! All!" he repeated soliloquizingly. "Oh God!" he then said, turning his eyes upwards, "God all-merciful! God all-good! help, help poor Irelan'!"

Both the Master and myself bent our heads, and I in my heart joined with Father Dan in his piteous appeal.

"Ay," said the Master in a low voice, "God help her! God help her!"

After a short while Father Dan spoke again, saying:

"Ay, Dinny. Ay, Dinny. I know it. I know it well; and forgive me. There's a few of ye leave us of your heart's free will. And them leave us never forget us.—Never forget Irelan'."

"Father Dan," I said grimly, "I'm one that 'ill never forget—never!"

Father Dan turned upon me eyes overflowing with kindly pity. And the Master looked at me in like manner.

"Two things," Father Dan said, still keeping his eyes bent upon me, "our poor boys and girls always carry with them, when they must go, and always bear with them though they go to the ends of the earth, and ever keep warmed in their hearts—two things; their religion, and their love of Irelan'."

"So," the Master said, solemnly, "it is so."

Father Dan did not lift his eyes from my countenance. He said:

"Whoever sees your heart, Dinny, sees that it's sore at the thought of leavin' Knockagar?"

I merely bowed my head.

"And your Uncle Donal—how is he takin' it?"

"Badly, Father Dan. My Uncle Donal's heart 'ill break if God doesn't sthrengthen him."

"Trust in God, Dinny," he said, aggressively.

"And I do trust in Him," I said calmly.

"Then ye'll have your reward, my boy," the priest said.

"It's a long time now, Dinny," he went on, "since the Masther begun showing ye off to me as his cleverest boy. We were just talking of that. And we were thinking what a crying pity it is that a lad who stuck to his books like you, and who picked up the good education you have picked up, should have to go to America, and slave with his two hands."

"Better than me did it, Father Dan. And my little education 'ill not make work any harder."

"Brave fellow," said Father Dan, admiringly. "Tell me," he said, "what did ye ambition being, now, when ye were hard at your books?"

I smiled confusedly, and did not answer him.

"Come, Dinny, tell me."

"Oh, many's the foolish notion comes and goes in one's head," I said, evasively.

"But I demand that ye'll tell me, Dinny. The Masther here has been telling me you used to have dreams of being a schoolmaster yourself?"

I was a little bit vexed that the Master should be parading my childish notions. With the air of one who puts his back to a rock and cries "Come on!" I replied, "And so I used!"

Father Dan's face gradually relaxed in a smile. But whether he smiled at my manner, or at the absurdity of my ambition, I could not say. The Master, I saw, was smiling, too.

I cast down my eyes, confused and confounded.

"Well, well, Dinny," said Father Dan encouragingly, "and sure, that was no harm."

"Dinny," he said, "ye've been getting no end of presents these days, I'm told."

"The neighbours' kindness is very great, Father," I said, feelingly.

"It is, Dinny. It is. Poor though they be, they'd suffer to be a deal poorer, sooner than any one in afther days, in a far land, could say they didn't reach there hand to him with a parting token. God bless them!"

Both the Master and I said "Amen!" most fervently.

"And I suppose, Dinny," he said jocosely, "poor as I am ye'll be thinkin' I should reach no empty hand to ye, either?"

I said, "Father Dan, you have too much to do, without minding to give me a present."

"And consequently me present 'll be small," he said. "The Master here has been informing me that he's going to commit marriage with—it's no use keepin' it a secret now—John Burns's daughter, Ellen. He's closing his school, and, to provide for his increasing charge, is taking the Cornagreine school, which Masther O'Neill has left. You, Dinny, will please accept, as my little present, the key of your own school—now doubly your own.

Here it is, Dinny, my boy. And with me ask the good God in whom we all trust, to grant that this may be the key to prosperity and to happiness for you and yours. May God bless ye, Dinny!"

CHAPTER XXVII.

FIVE YEARS AFTER.

On a November night, five years later, returning from my school where I had gone in the evening to give directions about extensions and repairs which were then in progress, I dropped into Toal-a-Gallagher's. Susie was working over the fire, preparing the stirabout supper. Toal and an apprentice from Barnesmore, were industriously working upon their benches. Several of the neighbours, as usual at that time of night, were there. John Burns was giving Dinny Managhan, the cart-man, particular and detailed directions regarding an addition to his library, which he wished Dinny to purchase for him on the occasion of his next journey to Dublin.

"When are ye goin', Dinny Managhan?"

"Monday mornin', with God's help, meself and the mare and cart takes the road."

"And ye'll reach there on Sathurday night? I want ye to go diract to 'Thirteen Byrne Thirteen,' on Dublin Quays, and ax for 'Cobbett's History of the Prodesan Reformation.' 'Thirteen Byrne Thirteen,' remimber. It's the capitalest book I've ever read—Toal, it'll delight you.—'Thirteen Byrne Thirteen'—that's the signboard, Dinny, keep it in your head. Pathrick Blake, of Althacappal, he has a damaged copy of it. It was him lent it to me eight years ago last June. But he come and he sat with me the three days I was readin' it, for feerd anything would happen it, or that I'd let any wan take it away. And then he went home with it done up in a parcel when I finished. I vowed I'd get that book, some day. Only Pathrick always refused to tell me where it was to be purchased. But, last fair-day of Donegal I come across him, and he had a couple of glasses in him, and was exthra friendly and loose in the tongue, and, Dinny, he let it slip that the time he thravelled all the way to Dublin twenty-wan years ago, to see Lord Francis about spairin's in his rent, bekase of the death of his five cow bastes from elf-shot all in the wan saison, he wandhered intil a bookshop on the Quays to get a Missal that Father Dan sent with him for; and as good luck would have it, he come upon an abused copy of Cobbett, and by purtendin' he didn't want it he got it for elevenpence. He looked at the sign-boord when he come out, and it was 'Thirteen Byrne Thirteen,' was the sign. It's about a mountain man's call below the Four Coorts he says, and on the left-han' side of the Quays. Go to it, Dinny—to 'Thirteen Byrne Thirteen's,' and look for a copy. As regards the price, I allow ye to use your own discretion inside of fifteen pence. Here it is. Buy it, Dinny, by pretendin' ye don't want it, and ye'll get it chaiper. 'Thirteen Byrne Thirteen' mind, on the Quays, Dinny."

"That manes," said Dinny, "that the gintleman's name was Byrne, and his house number thirteen."

"I don' know—I don' know," John said. But the sign-boord, Pathrick told me, give 'Thirteen Byrne Thirteen' as the name."

"And if Byrne shouldn't be there now?" Dinny queried.

"To be sure he'll be there. What 'ud happen to the poor man?"

"But I say *if*?" said Dinny, who knew in his heart though that in Dublin change never came.

"In that case, stick your head in some of the neighbours' doors," John replied, "and ax where

"'Thirteen Byrne Thirteen' is gone till, or is there anywan now who sells 'Cobbett's History of the Prodesan Reformation,' that grand book."

"I'll do the best I can, John," Dinny said, as, after dropping the fifteen pence into his canvas money-bag, he drew the running string, rolled the ends many times around the neck of the bag, knotted them, and deposited the great purse in the inner breast pocket of his inside vest, and buttoned over it all his vests and coats.

There was silence in the house; for everyone had been profoundly interested in the purchase which John was directing. A knock at the door—an unusual formality in Knockagar, surprised all of us. The door opened and a straight and tall, handsome young stranger, of quite gentlemanly deportment entered, bidding, "God save all here!" "Yourself likewise, and you're welcome, sthranger," was replied by several. Susie wiped a chair with her apron and tendered it to the new-comer, who accepted it with thanks, and sat down.

He said, "Excuse the liberty I take, but I am an American who have just reached here, the native place, as I understand, of both my parents. They have been, for long, anxious that I should come here, amongst all the old neighbours and friends, of whom I heard them talk daily and nightly—"

"You'll pardon my impertinence," said Toal, whose interest was excited more keenly, if possible, than ours, "but might I preshume to request to know who ye are, sir?"

"I," said the stranger, "am an officer in the American army. I have for a long time wished to come here. I am anxious to learn particulars regarding my parents' old friends. Have you got a man known as the Widow's Pat among ye? and how is he?"

"This is me," said Pat, from a corner, speaking up for himself, "and I'm well and hearty, thank God, and you."

"That's him," said Toal, corroborating Pat. "He's as hearty as a deer on the hills, and happier. His orphaned niece, Nuala, is to be married two weeks from now, on this worthy young gintleman here"—I blushed and felt very awkward as Toal indicated me with his hammer—"Masther O'Friel, who is Masther of our lokial school, and is growing rich and prosperous, and has made his uncle Donal both prosperous and happy, with not a penny less nor seven or eight-and-twenty sterlin' pounds of the realm accruin' till him every year. Masther Whoriskey, his l'arned predecessor, who married the worthiest girl in the parish, Ellen Burns, is flourishin' in Cornagreine school, and is about startin' a classical Academy at his own home in the evenin's."

"And John Burns, the local tailor?" the stranger asked.

"Is, by God's grace, as happy as mortial can be in this worl'. Tell your parents so, and thank them from me," John himself replied.

Said Toal, "Tell them Matthew McCoort—they'll mind Matt—and Owen a-Slaivin, is as happy as the day's long, and Corney Higarty—"

"Ay, Corney Higarty?" said the stranger.

"Which is me," said Corney, "is—as they say in the Amiriky letthers—well, and doin' well, only not makin' a big throw of money—but as contented, say, as a mouse in a cornstack."

"Tell your parrents, young man," Toal said, imposingly, "that Toal a-Gallagher—which is me, and Mistress Shusie Gallagher—which is that venerable lady stirring the pot, has both been doin' remarkably well, and would be happy out-and-out if they only could get thrace of a wild boy of theirs that, without provocation, left them seven years ago, and run off till the States."

"And you had an apprentice, a great handball player? His fame reached to the States."

"The Champion handball player then, and now, of the three Baronies of Banagh, Boylagh and

Tirhugh. Yes, sir, William Brogan was my apprentice. He is now Messrs. William Brogan and Company, Leather Merchants, Boots, Shoes, and Family Provisions—ye can read the sign for yourself, where he occupies wan of the finest establishments, and does the first trade on the Diamond of Donegal town. William came intil a large legacy which he got be raison of a millionaire uncle of his, worth hundreds of pounds, who died in Philadelphy. If ye remain here long—as we hope—and don't care to go intil Donegal to see him, ye'll have the pleasure of meetin' William Brogan and Company in a fortnight's time, when he comes here to act as Best Man to Masther O'Friel there, and Nuala Gildea. And ye'll likewise have the pleasure of seein' William Brogan and Company, on the Sunday evenin' afther, contestin' to houl' the lokial championship for hand-ball play, against Tim Griffin, of Glen Ainey, who has challenged William—and lost—every year of the past six. William's a bachelor, and goin' to remain ever so, he says. He stands sponsor for all the youngsthers of the country.—But, will ye be honourin' us with your company till then? And might I preshume to ax the name of your parents, young gintleman?"

"I'll be remaining till then," the stranger replied, "and a while longer. My parents were both, as I said before, natives of this place—they are named Toal and Susie Gallagher. I was called Toal, after my father, but was more generally known by the title of the Vagabone."

THE END.

BALLADS OF A COUNTRY BOY.

The Poems of Seumas MacManus.

"A Book to cherish, to smile over, and weep over by turns, is 'Ballads of a Country Boy.' . . . We meet here all the characteristics that have made of Ireland a great and holy nation. . . . Seumas MacManus shares with Ethna Carbery her magnificent sensuousness of imagery, and haunting melody of versification. The poems of both stand for what is most distinctly national, and, in a literary way, most excelling, in recent Irish verse.'—*The Leader, San Francisco.*

"It would be hard to find a new volume of popular poetry which excites one's interest from beginning to end to the same degree as these simple ballads of Seumas MacManus. Here we have the joyful, the sorrowful, the beautiful, and everywhere the interesting. . . . We feel our hearts glow, then, with a deeper love of Ireland."—*New Ireland Review.*

"This book is full, to overflowing, of love of Ireland, and Donegal, and the birds, and all the beautiful works of God"—*Irish Monthly.*

"What pleasure it gave me, with its lilt fresh from the hillsides of Donegal, and its blithe spirit brave and glad, alike in storm and shine! I have looked into it again and again since first I read it, and never without pleasure, or the sudden sense of wind and air, and the singing heart."—*Fiona Macleod.*

"The melody of song-birds, the perfume of Irish flowers, the soft light of Irish skies, and the pure passion and haunting melancholy of the Celtic heart are in these Ballads."—*The Pilot* (Boston, U.S.A.).

"Than Seumas MacManus no other writer holds closer communion with the mind and life and soul of Ireland. I have read this book three times over with increasing enjoyment."—*Sligo Champion.*

"The richest words are but poor interpreters of our feelings. I realise this as I close Seumas MacManus' 'Book of Ballads'; for what I wish to say I cannot express; but something clings around me and remains."—*Ireland's Own*

"His strains are on the lips, and in the hearts, of the men and women of his race."—*Gaelic American.*

"Joy and sorrow, life and love, passion and music, are in his lines. And it is evident that he has sung, not for mere effect, not for fame, not for money, but to console himself."—*Leinster Leader*

"Every Irish man and woman should have this book, it will cheer and sadden them by turns, as our dear land itself smiles and cries to us through all the ages." —*Catholic Herald*

"They are the best expression of Ulster poetic sentiment that have appeared since Ethna Carbery's gem-like verses first delighted the reading public.—*Irish News.*

"In turns, sad, tremulously pathetic, humorous, and impassioned, all the Ballads are characteristically Irish, and characteristic of a writer who never seems to miss the leading road to the hearts of our people."—*The Wexford Free Press.*

"There is not a Ballad in the entire collection that does not contain the true poetic feeling of a writer who writes straight from the heart."—*The Roscommon Messenger.*

"His song is of a sweetness and sincerity all his own. It is high praise of these Ballads to say that they are not unworthy of their dedication to the memory of Ethna Carbery."—*Northern Whig.*

"He gives us of his skill and genius imperishable gems of rarest beauty and excellence."—*Galway Express*

"One hears in these Ballads the trill of the birds, the crooning of the brooks, the murmur of the sea, the tinkling of the heather bells, the triumphant call in great days and deeds afar"—*The Derry Journal.*

"Here are all the passionate, beautiful, and purest qualities of our race."—*The Kilkenny Moderator*

"These are Ballads to inspire high and noble thoughts; to awaken new hopes for Ireland, and to keep love of home burning warm and pure and bright."—*The Meath Chronicle.*

Price 6d. paper; 1/6 cloth, gilt lettered; postage 2d.

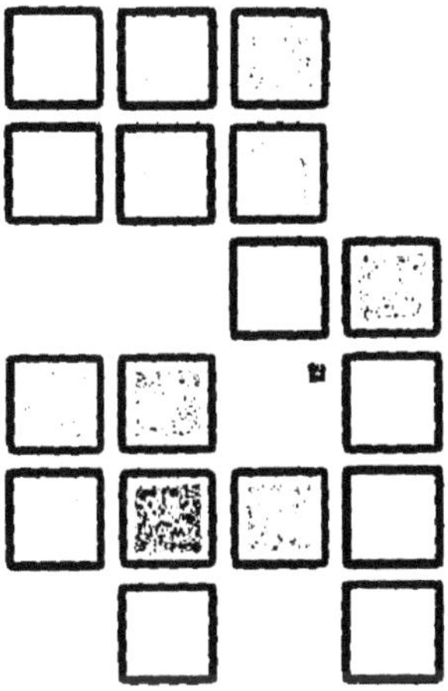

Lightning Source UK Ltd.
Milton Keynes UK
UKHW020002270521
384429UK00005B/1265

9 781371 426675